MW00442050

Anne Maggs

I NEVER DIED BEFORE

A Survival Guide to Aging and Beyond

LUMINARE PRESS

WWW.LUMINAREPRESS.COM

I Never Died Before: A Survival Guide to Aging and Beyond
© 2018 Anne Maggs

All rights reserved.
No part of this publication may be: reproduced, stored in or introduced into a retrieval system, transmitted, in any form, or by any means (electronic, mechanical, photocopying, recording, or otherwise), without the prior written permission of the author. Your support of the author's rights is appreciated.

This is a work of fiction. Names, characters, places, and incidents either are the product of the author's imagination or are used fictitiously, and any resemblance to actual persons, living or dead, business establishments, events or locales is entirely coincidental.

Printed in the United States of America

Cover Design: Melissa Lund

Luminare Press
438 Charnelton St., Suite 101
Eugene, OR 97401
www.luminarepress.com

LCCN: 2018909980
ISBN: 978-1-64388-004-4

*In memory of my parents, Bill and Anne,
who showed me that the way you encounter
death affects those who love you.*

TABLE OF CONTENTS

DEAR READER

Using many sources, I researched the material in this book for myself; however, I wrote the book for you. I did so to pay forward all the benefits I gained from learning about aging and dying.

This is not a book about healthy living; this is not a book about living longer; this is a book about aging with courage.

After retiring from a cherished career of teaching college classes, I turned my attention to learning about life after retirement. Back then, I was very naïve about what lay ahead. Old age seemed far in the future after years of leisure. I thought old age was a time to be shunned, even to fear. But what I learned from my research transformed my thinking. Now I live every day with curiosity and acceptance for what lies in wait for me.

This novel introduces information and guidance tips gathered from many experts. The companion journal exercises are designed for you to implement the tips into your own life. A physician once asked me, "Do you have someone who will speak for you in these matters?" I nodded yes. "Have you spoken to them?" At that moment, I realized that I had not. The exercises are my attempt to remedy that for myself and for you.

We are often competent at preparing a will to insure our wishes after death or perhaps an advanced directive for dire circumstances; however, we do not prepare our life for the stages before dying. We do not prepare for decline, for disability. We think we will just die at home at some unknown day in the future. You will discover the trade-offs of that approach by reading the advice columns and working through the exercises.

The Good Shepherd Psalm describes life as a walk through the valley shadowed by death. Aging is that part of life's journey where the landscape starts to change as you come under and into that shadow. This educational novel is a guide to help you plan your route and see the markers along life's trail that alert you to accommodate a change, to take a turn, or to stay your course.

I believe that aging is a gift to prepare us for crossing over, for passing on, for dying. I came to realize that how I die makes a difference to me and to those around me. The details of my dying will be what they remember. I seek good aging and a good death that is commensurate with my good life.

Anne Maggs

I Join the Editorial Team at Yew-Wood Mansion

At 72, I was the youngest member of the team. But, right now, I felt like the oldest as I struggled to push my fat-tire bicycle up the gravel path leading to the big mansion.

I was going to be late on my first day! Even though I lived close by, I had overestimated my ability to ride to work. The forgotten feeling of stress flooded back as I panicked to control the bike and myself. Thankfully, the gardener's apprentice, Ricky, was trimming the hedge along the path. I had met him yesterday during my orientation tour and he seemed like a very nice young man. Seeing my distress, he grabbed the handle bars from me waving me toward the big steps. "I will take care of this and you go-go-go. Don't be late! The others are already here and Lady Alyce never forgets a first impression."

I entered through the big oak door directly into a large foyer in the shape of an octagon. I hung my coat on an old, scrolled rack and glanced to my right up the sweeping staircase, admiring the beautifully carved banister which was mirrored by a modern stair lift mounted opposite it. Looking straight ahead down the hallway, running from the front to the back of the house, I caught sight of a maid scurrying into the kitchen midway down the right hand side of the hall. Off to my left was the front parlor where I could hear several voices talking quietly.

I smoothed my white blouse as I slipped into the parlor where Minnie, who actually was the oldest member of the team, was seated. She beckoned me with her frail, freckled hand and patted the worn velveteen settee, signaling that I was to sit next to her. I recognized the young woman hovering nearby, because I had been introduced to her and her twin sister the day before. Adrienne, in her crisp maid's uniform, handed me a saucer and cup and wheeled the tea cart next to us. I settled down just as the stair lift in the front hallway clicked to a stop. Carmen, in a matching maid's uniform, arrived promptly with cane in hand and helped a heavy-set, older woman to a wide-bottomed slipper chair stationed across the room from us. *She must be Lady Alyce*, I thought as I sipped my tea.

At that moment, a tall man in a dark suit strode into the room to stand in front of the intricately carved fireplace. His hard leather shoes clicked on the tiled hearth and Lady Alyce called out, "Lee, get off of the stone—those shoes will scratch it!" Chagrined, he stepped forward putting his black briefcase on a small side table. At that moment, I knew who was in charge.

I had heard that Lady Alyce had a lawyer nephew who managed her affairs; we were gathered today to hear his report. He got right to work by introducing me as Maggie—which was my nick name. He explained that I had been added to the team to help out with the mail generated by the advice columns that Minnie and Alyce had been writing. The overwhelming response to their first two columns had been completely unexpected. The newspapers were complaining because they ended up receiving inquiries and fan mail. Something must be done to redirect the responders. Evidently, in his eyes, my job was primarily to manage the mail problem.

I hoped I had been hired foremost to help write the advice columns. Because Lady Alyce and Minnie were in their 80s, I presumed I was to represent the 70-something point of view; the mail issue was supposed to be my second responsibility. Lee went on to explain that his manager, Lori, would be our contact person and she would decide when to get in touch with him as needed.

I had met with Lori the previous day for my interview. She was in a rush to find someone to start immediately and hired me on the spot telling me I would begin the next day, Monday. She gave me a quick tour of the mansion. As we took a whirlwind turn through the front parlor, she explained that I would be working for two older ladies who were striving to remain in the house and needed to make money to supplement their dwindling income. Lori described with begrudging admiration how they had cleverly approached the local newspaper to propose writing a series of advice columns called "Aging with Courage." They had sold their idea as a syndicated eight-column deal. But the unexpected volume of fan mail in response had become a pesky problem which ended up in Lori's lap. She wanted someone to manage the incoming flow, handle any complaints from the newspapers, and respond to individual letters as needed so she could focus on Lee's law practice and more important issues.

Holding up a couple of spreadsheets as props, Lee announced that the Board of Directors of Yew-Wood Estate was concerned that the deadline to donate the mansion to the city was fast approaching. However, they had agreed to allow Lady Alyce and her entourage to stay at the mansion for six more weeks.

Angrily, Lady Alyce said, "Tell them I will do as I please. Do NOT dictate terms to me. I only agreed with that proposal because you said it was the way to proceed with the Board. Do not forget, young man, that I am of sound mind and I will stay of sound mind. I will tell you when I am ready to let the city take over MY house. You cannot scare my staff with threats from the Board!"

Carmen immediately brought the smelling salts in preparation for what was evidently a predictable need for them. Lady Alyce waved her away and Lee hastened to smooth over his rough message. He made his apologies that he could not stay for tea and hurried out the front door and down the steps, briefcase swinging, phone already at his ear.

Quiet settled on the parlor as we sat still and waited for Lady Alyce to recover from her outburst. The morning sun flooded through the multi-colored pink and blue stained glass windows set high above our heads.

During my tour, Lori had told me the windows were the most valuable pieces in the house, as they were made in the early 1900s by a glass works studio called Povey Brothers, known as the Tiffany of the Northwest. She said the rest of the mansion was in disrepair; something was always breaking down. A real nuisance, she called it.

The great clock in the hallway ticked, the fan behind the gas fire whirred, and I could hear someone in the kitchen scolding Carmen for letting the tea go cold. Soon enough, Minnie went to Lady Alyce, stooping to pat her knee. "Come on Al, he's gone and we are waiting for your instructions. We have a new girl here and we need to set her in motion."

Lady Alyce roused herself with a shudder, calling out to Adrienne, "Get everyone together; tell Judy-Ray to come here. This is serious, call Oskar and Ricky in too."

We gathered there in the parlor, drawing the chairs into a circle, waiting for Lady Alyce to take charge. Surprisingly, it was Minnie who began speaking. "We need a plan. Lee has been here and he has given us a six-week reprieve from turning over the mansion. If we can keep the household together without asking for money above the budget, we should be able to focus on writing the advice columns. If we can sell our columns to even one more paper, we can make more money beyond the syndication deal." Turning her gaze on me, she continued, "But that is going to take a joint effort and the brains of our new helper here to think outside of the box."

Silence followed this announcement with an uneasy hesitation for what the Grande Dame would say. All eyes turned to Lady Alyce. Pulling her wooly pink shawl around her shoulders she said, "I want you to know that when I agreed to donate the mansion to the city, I didn't think we would be running out of money so soon. I think that sneaky Lee is cheating me." She sniffed into her hankie and dabbed at her eyes. Minnie interjected quickly in defense of Lee, "He tried telling her the costs were too high, but she was never good at the finances." *Hmm,* I thought, *the whole place must be in financial trouble.*

Every person there had a high stake in how Lady Alyce would respond—jobs were on the line. You could just about hear the wheels turning as we all waited to find out what would happen next. Ricky, whom I had met earlier on the garden path, glanced at Oskar with a quizzical worried look on his face. I had heard from Lori when she hired me that Oskar was the head gardener and had been with the two old ladies the longest. He was actually Ricky's boss but she said that he treated him like a son. The two young women, Carmen and Adrienne, nervously fiddled with their apron strings. Judy-Ray, who was the cook, said "Lady A, you can take back your promise to provide for me—I'll go live with my daughter if need be." Oskar chimed in with a quick smile, "Same here boss; don't worry about me."

I realized that the young women must have been new to working at the house since Adrienne didn't seem surprised with Carmen's question. "Is it time for us to start looking for work somewhere else?"

"No!" insisted Minnie. "We have a two-part plan in place with our special tea parties and our advice columns. You girls were hired to help us with the Monday and Wednesday tea parties and we need to keep doing them. So far, we have had good success. Judy-Ray, how much money have we saved up?"

"Only three hundred dollars profit so far. I am going back to the kitchen to keep baking. You all figure it out and tell me when I have to do something other than cooking. In the meantime, let's get going. Carmen we have scones to make. Adrienne, get the rooms set up for this afternoon."

Oskar and Ricky stood with hats in hand before Lady Alyce. In his deep reassuring tone, Oskar said, "We will stay on budget and fix that broken furnace ourselves. The cold weather is not over yet so we need to get on it." Lady Alyce nodded for them to go and beckoned me and Minnie to slide our chairs closer.

She seemed buoyed by the action around her. "That Lee cannot make us do his will. We shall persevere!" I glanced over to see Minnie grimace at this declaration. "Maggie, we are counting on you to keep the advice columns going. We have a deadline every Friday. Do you think you can do it?" *Good grief,* I thought, *this is a mess and it's only my first day.*

Minnie gestured for me to follow her and we wound our way from the front parlor down the long hallway and past the butler's pantry on our right. I glanced in to see its built-in cabinets showcasing all manner of colorful teapots and china tea cups. Passing by the kitchen, she called out to Judy-Ray that we were going to the basement to get started. *On what?* I wondered.

At the very end of the hall was a tall door that resisted Minnie's pull. "The house is settling," she explained as she tugged on the round door handle. Down the dimly lit, narrow steps we went and came into a surprisingly large, bright space with daylight pouring through a wide arched window. I realized that we were in the lower level of the mansion where the big stone foundation was cut into the sloping hillside overlooking the treetops of the gardens below.

Dominating the center of the large room was an old oak conference table. Piles of mail were spread across it; they were grouped into bunches and labeled by date. "These all came in the last ten days," she said. "We gave up trying to respond and simply tried to keep them by date, although I don't see how that helps us now."

Minnie gathered her long checkered skirt to the side and lowered herself into one of the office chairs pulled up around the table. "When the tea is over today, I want Adrienne to show you what she has been up to on that computer. She is a quick study and is wasted as kitchen help, but we need to keep trying to implement our original plan to hold two weekly afternoon tea services if we want to stay in good standing with the Board. Adrienne will be free in two hours; in the meantime you look through what is here and in the email account she set up for us. Once you know what we have done, you might be able to help us decide what to do next."

Accepting that she knew more about what was going on than Lady Alyce, I nodded my agreement. She hoisted herself up and started moving toward the stairs. "Do you need help?" I asked. "The most important way you can help," she answered, "is to ease Lady Alyce's worry by making those columns into moneymakers. We need to do something to keep the place going until Al is ready to leave. Lee wants her in assisted living, and I am beginning to agree with him as the stairs to the upper bedrooms, even with the lift, are taking it out of her."

I watched as she pulled herself up the narrow staircase, using the double rails which had been installed along both sides of the stairs. Waiting until she closed the upper door, I began to explore.

The big room seemed recently renovated into a pleasant work space lined with file cabinets and shelves full of ledgers, photo albums, and books. The thermostat had a warning, "Do **NOT** change this setting! Ask Lady Alyce!!" The readout was a cool 68 degrees. I buttoned my long wool sweater as I began to inspect the files. Quickly I realized that I was looking at the archival history of the house. From its blueprints to pictures of its occupants, from yellowed newspaper articles to old scrapbooks, from legal contracts to correspondence—someone had been an avid collector of information.

Finally I turned my attention to the leaning stacks of mail. As I began to slice open each envelope I became aware of the patter of feet above me in the dining room. *They must be serving tea*, I thought as I organized the letters, pulling them from their envelopes and stapling them together. I didn't know what I needed to keep, so I kept everything for now. I had once heard a wise teacher say that when you are tinkering, don't throw anything away until you've finished the project.

I must have been at it for awhile as Adrienne showed up long before I expected she would be free from helping with the afternoon tea. With a bright smile she said, "I see you dug right in. We had a system, but Lady Alyce stopped us part way through." With a knowing smile she added, "She does that a lot—the older she gets the more she is losing it."

Stifling my retort to her impertinence, I had the good sense, instead, to ask her to give me a summary of what she thought needed to happen now. "Well, the two old ladies are a constant worry to Lee, who is trying his hardest to help them. Lori hired us because he tries to mollify his Aunt by letting her try out her crazy ideas—like holding afternoon tea ceremonies. But as you already know, he is clamping down because they have frittered away so much money.

"Ten years ago, Lady Alyce and her brother, Lee's father, signed a trust agreement that donates the mansion to the city along with an endowment to care for it. The old man died years ago, and Lee really, really wants to fulfill his last wish. But Alyce is living too long and dipping into the money slated for the trust. Lee is afraid the city will not accept the old house because they will have to pay for its repair and upkeep."

"So you and Carmen were hired to help with the teas?"

"Yes, we both go to the university and this job fits with our class schedules and it gives us housing which is very expensive in this city. We have a room in the back with a separate entrance and our own, very small bathroom, which is okay because we sisters have shared worse spaces before. Carmen just started the nursing program so she is the upstairs maid helping Lady Alyce with her many complaints and hissy fits. I am one year ahead in school than Carmen and a business major. I plan to go on for my MBA degree and I will do anything to stay on course, even take a job as the downstairs maid."

Moving confidently to the head of the table, she plopped down and took off her apron, folding it carefully. "I am supposed to be helping Judy-Ray, but the challenge with the columns is much more interesting to me. I want to help you with that. Lee told us you would be in charge of them."

"You seem to have Lee's confidence."

"Oh, I don't really; it's just that the downstairs maid hears everything."

I will remember that, I thought as I pulled over a large pad with lined paper in preparation for an exercise I had used when I was a business professor, long before my retirement and years before my recent return to part-time work.

"Here's an exercise that will help us make some decisions. I will ask and you answer, okay? Number one, what is the status quo—what do we have here?"

Adrienne cocked her head, thought for a moment and said, "Actually, I think we have an opportunity hiding behind the problem of the mail. I say we should create a website and, in addition to the newspaper, post the advice columns online to see if we can get a big enough audience to support advertisements. We were all surprised—including Lee—that those silly columns Alyce and Minnie started off with were popular."

Nodding my head in agreement, I said, "Number two, what is the problem with how things are?"

"Well, the newspaper that originated the columns contacted Lee asking him to post a mailing address so that people would stop sending fan mail to the syndicated papers that run the columns. They can't be bothered by it. But Lady Alyce doesn't want anyone to know her location. As soon as we heard there was a problem, I set up an email address and posted it on the second column along with a PO address at the local Mailbox store. So, now we are getting both emails and letters. The emails are not a problem; I just go in and check them online. But the letters are piling up."

She is a quick study, I thought, then asked, "How many people are responding by email and how many by snail mail?"

Adrienne thought for a moment and said, "Hmm seems like half and half."

"Number three," I said. "Did the change solve the problem?"

Adrienne took her time to answer, finally deciding to make her pitch. "Yes, I think the PO Box and the email address are enough to keep the mail away from the papers. But I say we should take advantage of this opportunity that has dropped into our laps. We should identify the repeating themes from the letter writers and focus one of the remaining six columns on each theme."

I could tell that Adrienne had been thinking this through because she was excited to try her idea. "We could bring together a panel of students and faculty from the university who are studying the aging process and get a whole lot of viewpoints. Then you and I could synthesize the information for a column and put it out under Lady Alyce and Minnie's names. That way we would be offering valuable information instead of only their opinions. We would be the new editorial team."

Nervously, she waited for my answer.

Hit with the full force of her youth and ambition, I suddenly felt very old. Nodding but reluctant to face the implications of this much work, I said, "You think like an entrepreneur. I agree with you that there is value here for these readers." I swept my hands over the table with its piles of letters. "Whether or not we can make money from it is a completely different question."

At that moment, we heard Judy-Ray call for help.

Adrienne's idea was sound; she was onto something and I knew it. "Okay, I will put together a proposal for Lady Alyce that involves you helping me. Do you have time for that?"

Standing up to go, Adrienne carefully ducked into her starched maid's apron and ran her fingers through her short, curly black hair; "I do and I can use the exercise for one of my classes which will free up time I would have spent on a different project." Heading for the stairs she called out, "I will make sure that Judy-Ray is on board—you can take care of the others."

Later that evening, I was home telling my 94-year-old friend, Ruth, all that had happened. I had come to town two weeks earlier to be with her as she convalesced after surgery. While sitting propped up in bed, she listened eagerly since Lady Alyce was a local celebrity and Ruth's family had a distant connection to her.

Ruth lived around the corner and over the bridge from the Yew-Wood Mansion. Ironically, her grandfather had homesteaded the original acreage. To survive the depression of 1893, he had subdivided the property, splitting it in two at the creek and keeping the smaller piece on the south side. The wooded piece had been sold to Alyce's grandfather and construction on the Yew-Wood Mansion began in 1894. Generations later, Lady Alyce had inherited both the mansion and the woods.

For Ruth's side of the family, fate dealt a different hand. After many subdivisions and sell-offs she ended up inheriting one small parcel at the tail end of a 10-space mobile home park that bordered the creek. There she lived in a 12 x 40 foot manufactured home designed for her. The small interior space had front to back hand rails and easy access to kitchen and bathroom. The tiny house was perfect for her, but really too small to accommodate both of us for long. I had come to help her convalesce but as her recovery was slower than predicted, my time with her stretched out. In the hopes of bolstering my own funds, I had decided to look for a part-time job which is how I ended up working around the corner at Yew-Wood Mansion.

Her eyes sparkled as she learned details of the goings on inside the house and its locally famous inhabitant, Alyce. We were both enjoying this change in what had become a boring routine as she recovered from her surgery. We talked long into the night exploring all angles of the puzzle the columns had created. By morning, I had a plan.

One of the unintended benefits of working part-time was a way to escape from the confines of Ruth's small house. I had already visited all of the public spaces the city had to offer; so when I had a chance I asked Oskar if I could access the downstairs workroom during the day. He told me where the hide-a-key to the back door was kept and said, "You will find that this old house provides for us in many ways."

I didn't really think about his comment until I showed up the next day, Tuesday, around noon. I had left Ruth in the company of her neighbor, Frances. Together they were working on opening and organizing the mail which I had brought home with me in a big box. I believed that our subject of aging with courage was popular and would attract interest, so I had given Ruth and Frances the task of writing down the addresses from the letters as well as picking out the topics most important to our fans.

I followed the gravel path past the front porch. It sloped down the hill around the building. Just as Oskar said, I found the key tucked behind a chunky piece of stone stacked by the back door to the lower level. I entered to find the big work room occupied by our three youngsters engrossed in their computers; the girls were doing homework and Ricky was playing a video game. They kindly welcomed me into their inner sanctum.

Quickly we fell into a conversation about Adrienne's proposal to bring together faculty and students as panelists for the advice columns. We all agreed this was a good idea as was creating a website. I suggested that in addition to posting the advice columns on the website, we could film the panelists and post a video of our sessions. Adrienne volunteered to ask for help from a classmate, Brad, who was working on an assignment of how to monetize a YouTube video. She said we could ask him to use our videos for his project and further the reach of the advice columns at the same time. Ricky immediately jumped on the idea, proclaiming he could easily do the filming since he had a tripod and video camera.

Adrienne agreed to be the point person to schedule faculty and students for our sessions. Carmen said she could fill in for Adrienne with Judy-Ray to free her up from the kitchen. Ricky said he would ask Oskar for time off to film the panelists. Amazingly, in one short meeting we became a team, energized by the project to keep the household together.

We created a master calendar and began to schedule what we called Brainstorming Teas with the hopes that the promise of a free lunch would be enough to entice our academic panelists. We had to hurry because the first panel would have to be the next day on Wednesday since the column's deadline was on Friday. Adrienne confessed that she had already approached a professor and two students in the hopes that her idea would fly with me.

My job was to convince Lady Alyce that our plan would be worth the loss of the second weekly tea ceremony in exchange for a private luncheon with a panel of experts. I thought I might have enough leverage to gain her support. Actually, we had no choice since Adrienne had already posted a notice that the advertised tea ceremony for Wednesday had been canceled. The best advice I got before I left was from Carmen who walked me to the door and said, "It's Minnie you are going to have to convince. She's the one who can get Lady Al on board."

THE NEW TEAM'S FIRST COLUMN:
Stages of Aging

Minnie was convinced when I promised to devote one column to the topic of how to decide when to move to assisted living. Once she was on board, Lady Alyce came around quickly—declaring the whole panel idea as her own.

Our discussion in the workroom, out of earshot of the old ladies, had led to unanimous agreement to begin our series with a question from a 70-year-old woman asking what to expect as she aged. We were eager to see if the viewpoints of our panelists would give us relevant information for our first column.

Lunch had been served and Adrienne took a seat as Carmen began to pour tea and Judy-Ray brought in the dessert tray. We had assembled one retired faculty member from the Physics Department and two students who were working on senior theses papers that focused on aging. Adrienne had made name tags for everyone which helped get the group chatting comfortably.

Our first panel discussion was about to begin and Ricky set the camera to record. I gathered everyone's attention by standing to say, "Thank you for coming today to help us gain insight from your varying perspectives. I would like our physics professor to begin by explaining what he thinks about the process of aging."

Joe looked like a retired professor; his silver hair was disheveled and his tan sports coat had worn leather patches on the elbows. His lined face lit up when he began to talk.

"I am going to start with general concepts and move to the specifics of your question." We all nodded agreement as the dessert tray began making its rounds and Carmen glided around the table to keep the tea cups full.

"In order to talk about aging, we have to answer the question—What is Time? Over many years of teaching physics, I have come up with a description that makes sense to a lay person. Let's just say that for our purposes here, time on Earth is what we are talking about. We all accept as a law of the Universe that a person is in only one particular place at one specific time, right? So, how do we measure a particular place and a specific time?

"For example, right now, we could describe our Earth address by using latitude and longitude coordinates. This grid system describes our position on the planet. In the same manner, we can use a system to describe our position's movement as the Earth rotates. Measuring the movement of our position on the Earth is one way to describe the passing of time. For example, if we use a sundial to see where our Earth address is in relationship to the Sun, then we have a measurement system called solar time."

Joe took a break to ask for questions. Ricky could not help himself; peeking his head around the tripod he asked, "How fast does the Earth rotate?" Adrienne shushed him, but Joe said, "At the equator, one thousand miles per hour."

Ricky said, "Why don't we feel like we are spinning around at a thousand miles per hour?" Joe answered by introducing a helpful metaphor. "Imagine you are sitting on a train which is traveling at 100 miles per hour. Sitting in your seat, you do not feel that you are moving—you have the illusion of sitting still—but you know the train is moving because the landscape seems to be flying by. Just as we sit on the Earth and feel as if we are still, so does the landscape of space—the sun, the planets, the moon, and the stars—seem to fly by in a great circular wheel of rotations and revolutions."

A general chatter broke out which I calmed down by getting him back on track, "Before we move on, Joe, I want you to explain how this relates to aging."

"I will just say that if you think of time as the continuous measurement of how many rotations your body travels on the planet, then you will have a true physical image to think about aging as the wear and tear of that ride."

Seeing our quizzical looks, he said, "Okay, look at it this way. Aging and dying happens to every living thing, but our interest is at the level of an individual person. Our question here today is how time affects aging. Even though we don't experience the feeling of movement, the very fact that we are alive means we are riding the rotation of the planet. One natural lifetime is determined by the rate at which a body begins to wear out and internal systems break down. How long a person can keep riding depends on their DNA and the quality of life decisions they make along the way."

Looking around the table, Joe declared, "The mystery of aging is not whether it will happen, but when will we reach our final stop!"

His admonishment set a somber tone which was broken by Carmen making the rounds with a new pot of tea. Ricky fiddled with the camera as Adrienne stood to introduce our next panelist, Victoria, who was working on her senior thesis. "Please call me Vicky," she said as she passed out a paper. The handout listed five stages of aging: Fragility, Decline, Disability, Failing Health, and Active Dying.

"I am here to report on a book that is the focus of my senior thesis. This book was written by Katy Butler and is titled *Knocking on Heaven's Door*. I selected this book because I think it offers a valuable model for the growing movement to treat aging as a natural process instead of a medical emergency."

Vicky brushed back her long dark bangs and said, "In 1969, Swiss psychiatrist Elisabeth Kübler-Ross defined five stages of grief that terminally ill patients experience upon hearing of their diagnosis. Her groundbreaking book, *Death and Dying*, revolutionized the way health care providers talked to patients because she was the first to articulate the emotional turmoil that results when a physician gives a terminal diagnosis to a patient. She listed the five stages of response as: denial, anger, bargaining, depression, and acceptance.

"I believe that Katy Butler has done something every bit as important as what Kübler-Ross did. Butler has given us the stages of normal aging. Unlike the situation of receiving a terminal diagnosis, most people experience aging as a normal process of progressively losing resiliency over time. Each stage of aging is a drop down from a former baseline that cannot easily be recovered in spite of wishful thinking to go back to life as it was.

"Unlike the dramatic grief-cycle that comes with a terminal diagnosis, natural aging is a slow period of adjusting to decreased resiliency. Regardless of a patient's chronological age, their body has a biological age which is a reflection of their ability to function normally. Old age is not a diagnosis, it is a gradual process peppered with medical issues which requires a long-term, adaptive strategy.

"Medical issues associated with aging often occur during Butler's first stage, Fragility. This is the point in aging when the harm of the procedure may outweigh its benefit. The medical profession is designed to keep patients alive at almost any cost. The patient—or their advocate—must be the one who decides whether or not to take the risk. Now, obviously in an emergency, the physician will make that split-second decision. That is why medical personnel are so insistent on having informed consent and a POLST form filled out before proceeding."

Carmen interrupted to say, "A POLST stands for Physicians Orders for Life Sustaining Treatment." Surprised by her own interruption, she apologized and bustled around to clear the table.

Vicky thanked her and continued, "I got interested in this subject when I took my grandpa to the emergency room where they diagnosed him with pneumonia. I was with him when the doctor rushed in. She asked if he had a POLST and he said yes, but it was home in the safe. "Do you know what it says?" she asked. He looked at me and shrugged. As she listened to his lungs, she admonished him, "I just need to know from you if I am faced with a split-second decision to either try to save your life or just let you die. What do you want?"

Vicky held up her hands, palms up. "I simply couldn't believe that a young doctor would be so out of touch to put it that way. Then, I realized that she is an emergency doctor in the middle of a flu epidemic and there were people in the hallways on gurneys. Obviously, she was overwhelmed. At that moment, I realized that I could focus my studies on how to empower patients and their advocates to be ready for these crucial decisions that might not be made in the calm of a physician's office, but might be in the chaos of an emergency room environment."

Our third panelist spoke up, "I thought that's what a POLST is for."

"Have you ever seen one?" asked Vicky. "They want you to describe when to stop treatment, instead of focusing on the risks versus the benefits of a recommended procedure. In this first stage of aging, Butler argues that a normal part of aging is to encounter life threatening conditions. This is to be expected. So you have to be on the lookout for a situation that is developing into a need for hospitalization or a treatment requiring general anesthesia. These two conditions represent scenarios with diminishing returns for older patients."

Then, she adamantly stressed this point, "The risk factors grow as resiliency lessens. The odds of a good outcome have to be weighed against unintended consequences that may result in leaving a patient worse off than the original problem. These decisions are rightfully up to the patient.

"The doctor's responsibility is to lay out the options and the possible benefits and risks. To make these sorts of considered decisions the would-be-patient must understand their own goals for aging. This is where Butler's stages become reference points. Each stage describes a deteriorating ability to recover." Here she stopped and held up her hand. Using her fingers, one-by-one she renamed the stages: "Fragility, Decline, Disability, Failing Health and, finally, Active Dying." Pausing to let her ideas sink in, she reached into her large brown purse, pulled out the book, *Knocking on Heaven's Door*, and passed it around the table.

"I have one last point that relates to our question of what to expect. Butler's story is based on her own experience of caring for her parents. In hindsight, she came to realize that every medical procedure that each parent went through—as well as their decreasing ability to function—changed their base line as a couple who had promised to care for each other. The couple-ship itself frayed as her mom attempted to care for her dad.

"At some point, Butler's mom could no longer manage as her own health deteriorated, but she was bound and determined to keep them both at home. This stubbornness became an additional impediment to her children's ability to help her. Deciding when to accept help is complicated for those who wait too long to downsize from a house they can no longer manage or who were taken by surprise without a plan for when an emergency intrudes.

"The lesson I am taking away from Butler's book is to put a plan B, C, and D in place when both parents are capable of doing so. Whether in a couple-ship or living alone, you should do it while you still can—sooner rather than later!"

I was keeping track of time and felt a need to shepherd us onward. Thanking Vicky for her presentation, I turned toward our third panelist. At my nod, he stood and introduced himself. "Hello my name is Uri and the book I am studying is by Victor Frankl." He held up a small paperback. "It is called *Man's Search for Meaning*."

Uri was a tall, very thin young man who wore a black yarmulke on his closely cut red hair. His loose fitting black jacket hung down almost to his knees. He had a deep voice filled with passion as he discussed the book. "This is an astonishing account of Frankl's time in the concentration camps during World War II. He was a professor of Neurology and Psychiatry at the University of Vienna when he was captured and imprisoned in 1942. He survived the horrific experience of the camps and lived to write about it.

"All during his incarceration his desire to make sense out of how his fellow prisoners reacted is what kept him going. Upon release, he wrote this book about his new theory of psychiatry—he calls it Logo Therapy. His theory is based on what he observed in the camps when a human being suddenly realizes that he has nothing left to lose but his life—when all else had been forcibly taken away from him. The mixture of emotions and apathy incapacitated some; others discovered a will to live. Frankl observed that the will to say yes to life occurred in those who found meaning in the senseless suffering they endured in the camps."

Pausing to explain, Uri told us that Frankl believed that to be alive is to be susceptible to suffering and that every person is vulnerable to the suffering that life can bring. Knowing this from his first-hand experience in the camps, Frankl came to believe that one way to survive is to find meaning in the suffering. He proposed that while no one can tell another his purpose, each is able to find his own way and accept responsibility for what he discovers.

Referring to his notes, Uri read to us from his research paper. "Frankl believed that the ability to choose one's attitude when facing suffering is the last and greatest human freedom. It is a kind of spiritual freedom that cannot be stolen. As a former prisoner, he realized that no one had the power to take away his choice of attitude. His call to action for us is to find a guiding truth to live by which will serve as a personal compass to help endure suffering. For example, a person who receives a terminal diagnosis might adopt an attitude of acceptance rather than denial to save his family additional grief."

Uri held the small book in his hands as if it were fragile. "You see, Frankl believed that meaning lies dormant in the situations we face in life. Our task is to unlock meaning by gaining understanding so we can determine what can be done with the lessons life gives us. I believe this is relevant for our topic of what to expect as aging moves us closer to death. We have the freedom to choose our attitude when faced with the predicament of aging."

Gesturing toward Vicky, Uri said, "This is the sort of intentional choice needed to contemplate how we want to approach our death—how to develop the plans B, C and D that Vicky was describing. I look at aging as a gift from God. I think this because, as our bodies fail, we know in our heart of hearts that we will die. Fear of that reality can overwhelm us. However, one who faces a fate he cannot change can rise above himself, grow beyond himself, and transform himself by rising to the challenges of his own death."

Uri paused, seemingly lost in thought. Realizing that we were waiting for him to finish, he said, "I believe that the way you die makes a difference. Those who love you will remember the circumstances of your passing. Acting with courage in the face of disability and death is a legacy to your loved ones when they face similar situations later in their lives. I will close with a quotation from our revered Rabbi Hillel, who lived long ago. He said, 'If I am not doing it, who will do it? If I am not doing it right now, when shall I do it? But if I am doing it only for my own sake, then what am I?'

"I cherish those words because they are a call to action to take steps sooner rather than later. I am putting them into practice by my decision to leave school to help my grandfather to manage his life and stay in his home." Adrienne and Carmen both gasped at his bold declaration to abandon school; Uri blushed fiercely as he sat down.

I thanked the panelists and promised to send them a link to the video. As the girls ushered out our guests, I joined Lady Alyce and Minnie in the front parlor where our clever Ricky had set up a remote monitor so they could see and hear what was going on in the back parlor. We were watching them all file out when I noticed Carmen slip a piece of paper to Uri. *Oh*, I thought, *she is reaching out to help him.*

We all gathered to debrief. Lady Alyce complained loudly that she and Minnie could not possibly fit all of that information into one column. "Too much information, too much!" she exclaimed. I reminded her that Adrienne and I would write the column and that she did not need to worry about it. Carmen patted her knee and explained that Ricky was going to post the video so fans could watch it as well as read our column in the newspapers and on the website.

"I was shocked that the young man would quit school to help his grandfather. Not a good choice," declared Lady Alyce. The general hubbub masked Minnie's muttered, "Well some people give up their lives to help those they love."

After complimenting everyone and promising to deliver a draft column by 10 am, I left for the day. Ricky sashayed out the door right behind me and said he wanted to walk me home. When I tried to turn him down, he said that Oskar insisted I not walk home in the dusk. Later, I was glad to have his company as the sidewalk leading to the bridge over the creek was unlit and the shadows were deepening. I took his strong arm and we threaded our way past the bushes. He gave me a mock bow when we reached my door, pulled up his hoodie, and waved goodbye.

Ruth and I pored over several drafts of my response to the question we had chosen for the column. She was as excited as if this were the first day of school and her first homework assignment. We summed up our conversation on a yellow legal pad and I climbed up to my sleeping loft to work on my laptop as she began her nightly routine. I was out of her way as she pulled herself along the hand rails built by design into the tiny home. I kept an eye on her activity below me to see if she was recovering her strength; we both feared a fall. I noticed she was very deliberate as she scuttled between the bathroom and her bed.

My mind churned as I mulled over all I had heard, sifting it into smaller and smaller chunks that would fit into our prescribed number of column inches. Exhausted, I finally settled on one draft and carefully climbed down the ladder-type staircase to begin my own nightly routine. Ruth was sound asleep, snug in her berth-type bed underneath the loft. She seemed so frail when I watched her breathing. I couldn't tell if she was getting better or had settled into a new normal.

Aging: what to expect?

Dear Lady Alyce and Minnie: I have just turned 70 and I notice that I am not as motivated as I used to be. Also, I spend a lot more time just to get going. I have aches and pains that I didn't notice before and my bladder rules my life. If I am feeling like this at 70, I worry about how bad it is going to get. What should I expect as I age?

—Feeling it

Dear *Feeling It*: You have most likely noticed that the 60s is the decade you go into looking one way and come out looking another. Well, once you cross into your 70s, **don't** use your chronological age as a benchmark for your behavior, but **do** pivot to use your physical resiliency as a gauge of what you can do. The more time that passes, the more wear and tear life puts on your systems. In the coming years, you will have very important life decisions to make and they will be based on how you want to manage this final stage of your life.

We recommend three steps to prepare for the journey. *First*, create several contingency plans to your current living situation if (and when) you can no longer handle the upkeep and maintenance. *Second*, examine your life experience to see if you know someone who has aged in a manner that you admire. As you face the challenges of declining abilities, you need to choose how to handle the consequences that will limit your life—having a good role model will help. *Third*, embrace your mortality. Begin a practice to strengthen those characteristics that will serve you well in this end-of-life journey. For example you might want to use deep breathing to calm stress and help you fall asleep at night. Daily, you should identify actions you take that end up sabotaging your efforts. Be mindful to stop those and pursue helpful actions. In essence, living your life fully for as long as you can requires courage, planning, and good decision making. Remember that old age is not a diagnosis but it is a life path that is simultaneously richly rewarding and fraught with unexpected pitfalls. Say *yes* to life and live it fully until you cannot.

Feedback and the Team's Next Attempt:
Stage One—Fragility

W e were excitedly texting each other with every new response on the most recent column. Ricky was monitoring YouTube, Adrienne was monitoring the website, Ruth and I were opening the mail. We were a hit! Carmen was encouraging us to widen our audience to address the many questions from caregivers we were receiving, but I wanted us to stay true to the original idea of an advice column for "oldsters."

Mid-afternoon Sunday, I was on my way to the workroom to discuss our next step when Oskar caught up with me on the downhill path leading around the side of the mansion. "Good morning Maggie. May I ask for a favor?" He beckoned me to follow him to the very back of the house where he and Ricky lived in the old bunkhouse built long ago for the many workers needed to keep up the gardens and paths during the spring and summer.

Then he asked, "I wonder if you will help me and take a look at this paperwork from Holt International? I notice that you are a problem solver, and I have a problem." I had heard from Judy-Ray that Oskar was trying to adopt Ricky who was a refugee from Cuba. Evidently, the process had been going on for many months well before Ricky started working at Yew-Mansion. I read it over but could not make sense of it.

Looking up, I said, "Oskar, I think you should ask Lee to advise you. Take it to Lori first. She is coming on-site tomorrow and she very much needs you to stay here to keep the place going, so you have a little leverage with her. Ask her to have Lee look at it as a favor—seems to me you need a lawyer's opinion." Smiling as I handed back the packet, I said, "Remind Lori that you can't afford one on the wages she pays."

Oskar directed me to go down the back hallway to the workroom where I heard loud music and voices. *Sounds like a party*, I thought as I knocked on the inner door. Immediately, the music was turned off and the door cracked open. Seeing that it was me, Carmen waved me in. I was surprised to see Uri there looking very comfortable. He and Ricky were intently playing an old Nintendo game they had found in the cupboard.

Adrienne gathered up her books as Carmen collected the cans and pizza boxes clearing a place for us to roll out the big spreadsheet I carried in with me. Previously, we had agreed to decide on the topic of the next column today so that Adrienne could reach out to schedule our next guests. Carmen had said she would make a lunch menu and work with Judy-Ray.

I began, "Shall we stick with the same plan of having three guests for lunch in exchange for one weekly tea?" Heads nodded all around—yes—everyone liked that idea. By now, Ricky and Uri had joined the girls who were poring over the large grid I had created to categorize the topics from the feedback we had been gathering.

"As you can see, I have started to organize the themes that we extracted from the fan mail. All of these below the middle line are from caregivers. The ones on top are from seniors. I think we should focus on the top ones." I was surprised with a chorus of assent. "Great! Now, look at how the questions progress through the stages of aging that Vicky told us about." They all nodded as I pointed out the headings: Fragility, Decline, Disability, Failing Health, and Active Dying.

"These stages are driven by the loss of resiliency to recover from illness—the more fragile the patient, the more difficult the recovery. As you can see from the questions I have written in each column, oldsters worry about issues that vary with each stage.

"For example, look here." I put my finger on the first column of the spreadsheet titled FRAGILITY. "See, the companion issues are loss of healthy baseline, inability to care for pets, and loss of loved ones."

Carmen was studying the sheet carefully. Putting her finger on the column headed FAILING HEALTH, she turned to Uri and said, "Your grandfather is right here." His eyes filled with tears as he nodded in agreement.

Smiling brilliantly, Adrienne said, "I like this sort of organization—good job! This gives us guidance for the next five columns. If we can keep putting together a panel and gathering information to publish, that could be a big help to people who are going through these stages."

Carmen added, "Even though we are not focusing on the caregivers, this information will help them better understand how to nurse people from the patient's point of view." She put her hand on Uri's shoulder, "We will help your grandfather and this will show us how."

Once we had agreed on a plan, we had much to do behind the scenes to get ready. Asking Judy-Ray to provide a full lunch was asking a lot because she was already baking for the weekly tea service as well as cooking for the household. She didn't seem to mind and was as excited about our success as were we. She stood with her hands on her hips with her stout legs firmly planted—her big apron already showing the signs of her famous cherry strudel. "Bring it on Maggie. Carmen and I can do it."

After much preparation, we were finally set to begin. Lady Alyce and Minnie took their places in the front parlor sitting close to the monitor that Ricky arranged for them to eavesdrop on the meeting. They snuggled their chairs in close together so they could see and hear. I heard Lady Alyce tell Carmen, "See, what a good idea I had to film the panelists!" Carmen *tsked* at her false boast as she spread a flowered quilt over the old ladies' laps.

Adrienne invited one faculty member whom I had requested from the philosophy department and two students who volunteered to share their senior papers with us. She said they welcomed the practice for their upcoming presentations at school.

As soon as the lunch dishes were cleared and the dessert tray was circulating, I stood up to introduce Dr. Collet. "Thank you for coming Professor Collett. Several weeks ago, I heard a presentation that you gave at the Episcopal Church. The topic was on living in a way that cultivates the sacredness of everyday life. As I mentioned in my email to you, these sessions on aging focus on the loss of physical resiliency. I am hopeful that you will focus on steps to strengthen our inner resiliency by what you called 'care of the soul.' Please begin."

Even seated, Professor Collett was an imposing man with a mane of silver hair and dark brown skin. His sharp gaze settled on me as he began to speak in a deep voice, "We all agree aging is a process. How is it different than life?"

For a second, I wasn't sure if he expected me to answer, but he continued, "Well, in an odd way it mirrors the first stages of our life, but in reverse. On the front end we are developing, and on the back end we are devolving. We begin as a completely helpless infant and some of us will end up that way as a helpless senior—I see it as one big cycle." He held up his hands to form a big "O."

"But here is something to think about; being helpless as a baby is survivable because it is coupled with ignorance—we don't know anything. When we are born, we have the potential to be conscious, but babies aren't ready, are they? Hundreds of thousands of experiences are needed to shape us even before we will have a conscious experience that will, in later life, become the first memory we can recall.

"All along we are evolving through the passages of life to learn how to function in our world, to restrain our impulses, to learn to love, to broaden our thinking, until we reach a point at the other end of the circle, where finally all the cards are on the table. There are no more to draw from. Even though we may end up helpless, we have the advantage of being conscious and a life-time of memories to draw on."

Our third panelist interjected, "True, unless our minds have gone before our life goes." A general chatter broke out with one comment ringing above the others. "Everyone worries about that!"

Dr. Collett nodded in agreement and thanked Carmen as she refilled his cup and he sipped the tea with delight. "If we retain our mental faculties, there will inevitably be a moment, when for whatever reason, we come face-to-face with our own mortality. Some will stay in denial, some will receive it with a whimper, and some will call it an existentialist slap. The human mind recoils from the bright abyss of our impending death. One of our panelists will talk more about that," he said, nodding to Phyllis sitting to his right.

"The talk that Maggie attended at the church was really a self-help program for the soul. It is a program to help people wake up to the need to strengthen that inner part of us that asks the big questions like 'what is the meaning of my life?' and 'what happens when I die?'

"Self-help means we seek to make the most of what we have in order to live our lives more fully. You know the drill: stay fit, eat healthy food, avoid this or that, keep your mind active, and so forth. In other words, live your life, but don't eat too much of the cherry strudel, no matter how delicious it is!"

We laughed at this because the strudel was making its way around the table for the second time.

"My point is that when faced with the fact that your physical body is expected to go through changes of the magnitude to cause death, you better get ready. We need to be strengthening our non-physical realm by building up our soul muscles, so-to-speak. You will be taking the most important final examination of your life, so preparing for it seems like a very good idea. A healthy soul will help you navigate the ups and downs of this final journey.

"The beauty of this practice to strengthen the soul is that you don't have to buy a special piece of equipment, you don't have to travel, and you don't even have to join a church. Although, if you are going to church then you are already working in the same arena that I am talking about. You do have to be mindful, to observe yourself, to be conscientious in your actions. My message is that the most important aspect to being alive is in how you handle the experiences life brings you. Care of the soul is found in the small deeds of kindness, the kindly thoughts for others, the gentle manner of companionship; it is found in the ordinary details of life.

"My advice to you right now—today—is to focus on the qualities of your character that you want to be remembered for and begin an intentional practice to deepen them. Strengthen your relationships, take delight in every day you are alive, love one another. I encourage you to find a place that is sacred to you; then sit in it and absorb the rare gifts of its holiness. Be open to the new experiences that an attitude which appreciates the sacredness of life will bring you." With this, he stopped, smiled and said, "Oh, and pass that strudel over here!"

The easy laughter which ensued was a good transition from the professor's message to our next panelist. She was an exceptionally tall girl with very long brown hair. *An athlete*, I thought as I introduced her. "This is Phyllis, and she is going to talk about that existentialist slap the professor mentioned."

She looked around the table with much confidence. I noticed that she had positioned herself to sit opposite the camera in the best angle available. She began by passing around copies of her paper, titled *My Bright Abyss: Meditation of a modern believer.* "This is the title of the book by Christian Wiman which I reviewed for my senior thesis paper."

Tossing back her silky hair, she began by telling of her life interrupted with a cancer diagnosis when she was only 17. Her exceptional height was linked to a problem with her pituitary gland. By the time they discovered that cancer played a role, the disease was threatening to take her life. She held up the dog-eared book and said, "This book was my companion through that awful experience. When Adrienne explained your project of the Brainstorming Teas, I said I wanted to be a part of it, because even though I faced death as a young woman, I have learned that the only difference between me and you," and here she turned to face me, "is that you will have many more years under your belt than I did when that time comes."

She began reading her book review, but I was oddly absent, my mind preoccupied by her singling me out. Of course she was correct, but to have this tall avenging angel of near-death experience point her finger at me was a reality check of my own mortality; it was my own existentialist slap.

Carmen's arrival with freshly brewed tea brought me back to awareness of the room, to the clinking of silverware and to the drone of Phyllis' continued reading from her report. "Wiman's own cancer diagnosis and the horrible pain of experimental and aggressive treatments led him to question and define his own belief system."

She lifted her head from her paper and said, "I found this to be true of myself. I did a lot of soul searching as I went through treatment. He said one thing that really activated me." She flipped through the pages of her report until she found what she was looking for. "Oh, here it is. 'What do you do, what do you say, what in the world are you going to believe in when you are dying?'—that was it for me. That was the question I wanted to answer before cancer took me over. I wanted answers so that I was ready to face it.

"He is a poet, so his writing is very dense and he asks a lot of questions. This is just the sort of book you want when you are waiting and waiting for either a treatment to begin or to find out results. The waiting is one of the worst parts of a life interrupted."

Giving up on reading her paper as she had planned to do, Phyllis began summarizing the book. "Wiman wrote this book for a secular audience, for those who continually question even the existence of God. So there is not a lot of consolation in here, but there is an affirmation for those who want a guide to being courageous in the face of death. However, for those who know what they believe about suffering and death and live their lives within a belief framework, this book is frustrating because he never lets himself relax—he keeps hedging his answers.

"I found out that pain could instantly shift my mind from a normal reality of living to an altered state of extreme focus. I could tell the doctors that, yes, I understood the risks. But when I was lying there waiting for the treatment to begin, I had only myself, only my mind to help stay strong. For all the loving support I had, in the end, it was up to me. I was the only face looking in the reflection of the scanner. I discovered that pain was physical but suffering was mental. So, I learned to pray for relief—not for a miracle—but with a furious pursuit of belief. I had a panting exercise I did, like the Lamaze ones they teach for a natural childbirth. One of the nurses showed me how to use the panting and deep breathing to keep my mind focused on relief."

Here she paused in one of those daydream moments where everything stands still—a little slice of eternity. With a shudder, she came back to us and said, "I found my answers."

We sat still out of respect, subdued with the pure power of her story. She was a living example of death's mysterious timing.

Just as I was about to move to our third panelist, there was a loud crash and a cry from Judy-Ray. Adrienne sprinted away followed closely by Carmen. Ricky shut off the camera and we all turned toward the kitchen to look, anxiously waiting to see what had happened.

Adrienne emerged, "Judy-Ray fell backwards off a stool. I think she broke her foot. I am calling 911. Carmen needs help." I signaled for Ricky to go and said to the others, "We should end our tea." Turning to our third panelist, I said, "Aamod, we will talk about a follow up interview, okay?" He nodded and everyone rose to gather their coats. As I shepherded them toward the front door, we glimpsed Carmen bending over Judy-Ray who was still on the floor but sitting up in the midst of broken teacups scattered out into the hallway.

I had forgotten about the old ladies in the front parlor listening in. By the time I had escorted our guests down the hallway, past the parlor, and out the big front door with reassurances and goodbyes, Lady Alyce was clumping her way back down the hallway toward the kitchen with Minnie close behind. Lady Alyce cried out, "Oh what a mess! Are you alright dear?" Minnie broke down in tears and clung to the doorway.

The general hubbub was silenced when the first responders arrived with a gurney which they expanded once they maneuvered Judy-Ray onto its sturdy bed. Carmen grabbed her coat, following them down the front path to the ambulance, so she could ride with them. Adrienne shouted out her promise to call Judy-Ray's daughters.

Oskar helped me settle Lady Alyce into the stair lift and walked beside her as she rose majestically up the curved staircase. I came along behind helping Minnie slowly climb step by step. I followed her into the first bedroom to rest and to debrief with the others. Adrienne arrived in a rush. She had been looking for the emergency phone number for Judy-Ray but could not find the employee files. Her frustration added unease to the disrupted household routine.

With a stern look that got her attention, I said, "Just call Lori to tell her what has happened and to ask for the number." Lady Alyce burst out, "No, don't let Lori know, she will tell Lee and that will put an end to our teas." Minnie pulled a small book from her housecoat pocket, "Here Adrienne, use this number." Typing the number into her phone Adrienne called out as she trounced down the stairs, "I'm going to the hospital—back later!" The front door slammed hard behind her. "Ouch," I said, and Oskar nodded.

Minnie turned down my offer to help, "We can still manage to get ourselves to bed," she said with a sad smile. "Our bigger problem will be what to do about meals while Judy-Ray is in the hospital, let alone what to do about the teas."

I reassured her that we would talk about it tomorrow and Oskar promised to bring up a light dinner later on, before he buttoned down the house for the night. Lady Alyce beckoned twice for Minnie to help her to the bedside. She snapped, "Straighten up before you start walking. Don't hobble around like that—you look like an old lady." Oskar grimaced at her unkind words and guided me out of the room.

We could hear Ricky sweeping up the mess in the kitchen. "Oh boy, she really took a hard fall trying to reach the cups. I guess we should have kept Adrienne helping her instead of working on the columns." Oskar patted my arm. Turning to Ricky, he asked if he would sleep on the couch tonight in case anyone needed help. "You bet," he said earnestly. "I will go get my gear."

We pulled up two stools to the kitchen side-bar. Oskar disappeared around the corner to the butler's pantry and returned with two crystal glasses and a bottle of brandy. "We need to get centered," he said holding up the bottle. I nodded my agreement.

Later, as I was telling Ruth of my day, I told her that sitting and talking with Oskar was the closest companionship with a man I had experienced since my husband died eighteen months ago. I realized that I missed the down-to-earth nature of a man's perspective. She agreed, "He is a good caretaker of the place, a good parental figure to Ricky and the girls, and strong support for the old ladies. If something happens to him it's game over. They will never be able to stay in that falling down house without his help."

Our conversation stirred up memories from that difficult time of depression I went through after my husband's death, when I seemed paralyzed with inaction. Finally, my neighbor, Ursla, came to shake me up. She said, "Enough is enough. You have grieved until you are like the walking dead. Come on, let's clean up this place." We had lived in a big home which we had made into our sanctuary after years of fruitful careers. I knew I needed to face the fact that somehow, I had to burrow my way out of its suffocating influence to live in the past.

Ursla was Swedish and she told me they had a custom called "Death Cleaning" which was a methodical process to shed the baggage of life. She volunteered to get me organized and started on the journey of downsizing. *Thank God for Ursla*, I thought as I looked around at Ruth's minimalist home.

Ursla had worked with me for many months to sort, organize, and disburse. We had approached the task by looking forward rather than back. We imagined me in a new, small house. Using that as our goal, we selected only those items that I would need and some I simply could not part with. Once those decisions were made, she was a whirlwind of activity in setting up garage sales, dump runs, trips to St. Vincent de Paul's donation drive through, and the senior center. We packed many boxes into the POD mobile storage unit sitting in the driveway. One of the most important steps we took before we began was to take a detailed video of each room while it was still intact. I anticipated many hours of pleasure in watching this video when I wanted to revisit my old home.

Close to the time we were finishing, I had a call from Ruth asking for my help after her surgery, and I had agreed to come live with her for a short time. Ursla and I finished up and we had the POD container taken to their site for long-term storage. She told me that she had enjoyed the distraction from caring for her own husband and used the money she made to hire caregivers so she could have a break. She agreed to take care of my two kitties while I went on this adventure to help Ruth. My life was on hold, all packed up and waiting for my next move.

My reverie was broken off when I received a text from Adrienne that Judy-Ray's daughters were on their way to the hospital. She and Carmen would wait for them to arrive and then would head for home. She wanted to meet before noon tomorrow to discuss the column. I texted back my thanks for their effort and said I would begin a draft for us to look over.

We met mid-morning, but spent hardly any time reviewing the draft of the column on fragility. Adrienne had nothing to add except that we would need it early tomorrow, "Can you do it?" I assured her I could and that I would email it to what's-his-name's drop box. "His name is Brad. Once he gets it, he will post it. Ricky has already sent the film, but he edited out the loud crash at the end. I think it will be okay."

We spent our time looking forward by going over the spreadsheet. She put her finger on the subject for next week's column titled, Decline. "See these issues that seniors worry about, loss of home, loss of routine, and financial worries? Well these are the very ones Lady Alyce will face if she goes into assisted living. I know Minnie wants her to, but she would not be happy."

I was surprised with her opinion. "I thought Minnie wanted her to go because they could go together." Adrienne shook her head emphatically, "Nope, Minnie doesn't have the money and Lady Alyce would never settle on a low scale place. They should stay here where they have everything and where we can all continue with our work on the columns and Carmen and I can stay in school."

Aah, I thought, *the truth comes out.* I recalled in a flash those times she had silently manipulated Lady Alyce to believe that staying at the mansion was best. Minnie was simply outmaneuvered. *Not fair*, I thought gazing at her downturned head as she studied the sheet. Her glossy black hair was cut short revealing her classically shaped neck. Her long lashes hid her deep brown eyes. *She is an extremely beautiful girl*, I thought, *on the outside at least.*

We didn't know it yet, but our little world was about to come apart at the seams. Judy-Ray would not be coming back as her fall was the beginning of a series of setbacks that would put her into a long-term rehabilitation facility close to her daughters. The crew at Yew-Mansion would have to fend for themselves if they were going to try to stay the course. Not knowing what lay ahead, I wrote up our second column.

What just happened?

Dear Lady Alyce and Minnie: I have worked hard all of my life to be self-sufficient upon retirement. I have a very nice condominium in a homeowner's association where I live with my cat. I take great pride in not needing help. I manage my budget, live within my means, keep my house clean, and care for my precious cat. All of this was knocked out of kilter when I fell in the night and broke my hip. I lay on the floor for a long time before I could crawl to the phone to call 911. I just couldn't believe I ended up in that predicament. I am so angry that my body betrayed me. What can I do to make sure this doesn't happen again?

—Worried

Dear *Worried*: We can tell from your story that you are a capable person. However, you have been given a wakeup call by life. Now, you have to accept the fact that all you worked for to be self-sufficient later in life is no longer enough. A change is needed.

Even though your retirement seemed to be working just as you had planned, you had not calculated in the possibility that your body would give out. We think the most important first step is to move from this feeling of anger into acceptance. This requires an insightful examination of your values and beliefs. The pride you feel in not needing help has been destroyed by your anger. Your body is not to blame; it is simply reacting to the forces of aging. A better source of pride is one based on your own willingness to accommodate what life brings to you. However, this will require courage on your part.

Think about it. Your years of striving are over; now is the time to prepare yourself for this next stage of unexpected pitfalls. We simply cannot plan for a life where we never end up on the floor, so-to-speak. Instead, what you must do now is build a support network of friends and neighbors to call on in time of need.

Yes, there will always be professionals to call, but we are talking about that inner sanctum of life that is now inhabited only by your cat. Can you find others to cultivate relationships that are mutually helpful? This will require you to put yourself in situations you may not be comfortable with, like attending events to meet people, nurturing those acquaintanceships into friendships, being willing to help others in need, or even volunteering for a cause you care about. We believe that you can live a long time enjoying your retirement if you can adopt an attitude of accepting and giving help.

Can the Team Keep Going?
Stage Two — Decline

I had heard that Judy-Ray was going to be released today, so I was not surprised when summoned to the front parlor by Carmen who was twisting her apron strings nervously. But I was confused when she said, "The daughters are both here and they are mad and upset. Adrienne wants you to get rid of them before our guests arrive."

Today, we had convened a panel of representatives from different housing options for seniors. I had promised Minnie I would devote one advice column to assisted living and she was very keen on Lady Alyce hearing about her options. Also, I wanted to counter Adrienne's influence to stay in the big mansion regardless of whether it was good for Lady Al.

I hustled up the hallway and greeted the daughters who were in no mood for introductions, but I learned that the oldest, Susan, wanted answers about what had happened. The youngest, Linda, just wanted to make sure they picked up all of Judy-Ray's possessions. I took them both back to the kitchen where Carmen was trying to prepare scones and tea for the upcoming meeting. We had given up on serving lunch to our panelists; besides they were eager to tell us about their businesses so we didn't need to bribe them with a free lunch.

Susan and Linda stood at the doorway looking in as Carmen pointed out the high shelf where Judy-Ray had been trying to reach a tray of teacups. The small footstool was now tucked into its corner under the counter. The girls calmed down once Carmen said how badly we all felt and we missed their mom like crazy. Soon we were all crying as they told us that she had to go into rehabilitation for her shattered ankle; they wanted to move her close to their homes. Susan said, "She is so strong willed. We begged her to quit cooking for you guys and take it easy. But, as you know, she is very dedicated to Lady Alyce and to Minnie."

Linda chimed in, "She loved them and they knew it."

Carmen pulled open the drawers looking for anything that might have been

Judy-Ray's. I packaged up a beautiful china tea cup and saucer for them to take to her. "Remind her we will be praying for her and thinking of her when we drink tea," I said handing over the small package. Having vented their feelings, they left to go back to the hospital and we gave a collective sigh of relief.

"Whew, that was hard; we are really, really going to miss her," said Carmen. At that moment, my stomach flipped as panic filled my mind from thinking about the ripple effects of losing Judy-Ray. She had played a crucial part in us being able to pull off the Brainstorming Teas. *What are we going to do now?* I wondered.

Adrienne called out, "They are here!" Ricky flashed a thumbs-up as I passed by heading toward the door. Earlier, he had set up the monitor in Lady Alyce's bedroom rather than bringing her downstairs after her late-morning nap. Oskar had helped arrange a small desk in front of the couch in her suite. I knew they were comfortable and Minnie would keep them focused on listening to the panelists. As I went to the front door, I thought, *Thank God the old ladies were upstairs when the daughters came. They don't know Judy-Ray is not coming back.*

Pulling open the big oak door, I ushered our seven guests down the long hallway and directly into the dining room. This area was across from the kitchen which would cut down on steps for Carmen as she served tea. The big table was set with place cards because Adrienne had decided to arrange the seating to represent a continuum of care based upon a senior's needs. This created a visual example of the levels of care each business provided. The head of the table was HOME CARE, followed by COMMUNITIES, ASSISTED LIVING, MEMORY CARE, RESIDENTIAL CARE, and the highest levels of care: NURSING HOME and HOSPICE.

I was so distracted thinking about Judy-Ray that I could hardly focus on getting the meeting started. I waited until the scones had been passed around and the tea poured. Small dishes of clotted crème and lemon curd nestled beside each plate, although no one had done any baking; the pastry was from the market. What I saw laid out was the best we could do under the circumstances. *Judy-Ray would be disgusted with us,* I thought as I signaled Ricky to start the camera.

The sea of faces turned toward me as I cleared my throat. "As you know we are writing columns on aging." Yes, they all nodded; they knew that. I indicated Ricky's position directly behind Adrienne and said, "When you tell us of the services your company offers, you should turn toward the camera so that the YouTube audience can see and hear you." I must have paused too long because Adrienne cautiously picked up the thread of what I was saying, "As you can see the seating is arranged according to the level of care your business offers." Turning to the woman seated at the head of the table, she said, "Please begin."

Her choice to begin with home care was a good one. This woman was obviously skilled in quick, memorable presentations. Not only did we learn the benefits of home care but we also learned a rule of thumb about how to determine when and what care is needed. Every presenter after her referred to this criterion to introduce what their company provided. She said that both insurance companies and the government determined their benefits according to needing help in two of six areas. She handed out a small brochure with LIVING ACTIVITIES listed on the back: eating, bathing, dressing, toileting, transferring, and maintaining continence.

I saw Adrienne visibly brighten when the home care lady said, "Our service can be the right choice for seniors who want to stay at home and need only minor assistance. Higher levels or more frequent care is usually not practical or affordable."

To her right was seated a young Indian man who spoke with a British accent. His place card showed that he represented COMMUNITIES. His expensive suit and impeccable grooming signaled he would be representing the costly end of the choices available. "Thank you so much for inviting me to your lovely home. I am especially grateful to be here with colleagues whose businesses are working to provide our esteemed seniors with many choices during the golden years of their lives." He talked about his company which brokered placement with independent living communities ranging from activity-focused seniors living next to golf courses, more sedate senior estates with walking paths, or senior apartments that offered the help of professional staff for maintenance and beauty salons for personal care.

As I listened to his voice rising and falling in the wonderful cadence of the Queen's English, my mind wandered to thinking of Ruth and how she had ended up in the tiniest of houses around the corner from the big mansion. *She's happy there*, I realized as he wrapped up his presentation.

Adrienne transitioned the conversation by pointing out that both speakers so far offered solutions that were for healthy, independent seniors. Her comment caught my attention. I knew that Lady Alyce prided herself on being independent, ignoring the fact that she had both Carmen and Minnie helping her; she insisted to Lee that she did not need help. *Oh—Adrienne is playing to the audience upstairs*, I thought grimly.

As she introduced the next speaker, she commented that the remaining options were for dependent seniors—those needing help with two or more living activities.

The next speaker was a friendly, ex-nurse who assessed seniors to see if they could manage in an assisted living facility. Her assessment of the six living activities determined the level of placement. She worked for five different businesses that provided differing levels of care. She explained that almost all of the facilities offered help with medication plans, meals, housekeeping, and any individual care needs. She passed around an attractive brochure showing the small kitchenettes that were typical in a studio apartment. She explained that each apartment had a call button which summoned staff who were on duty 24 hours a day.

Adrienne broke in, "Oh, but those rooms are so tiny."

Looking around at the beautifully furnished room, the nurse said, "Our dining rooms are not quite this elegant, but they are filled with residents who come to share meals together. There are many social events planned with movies, special field trips, and clubs for seniors to socialize. I have one home that takes pets and one that specializes in lectures and travel films. Our mission is to create a caring community focused on our residents. We are there to fill in where they need help, to listen, and to value their life experiences."

When our next guest began to speak, I realized that we had switched from talking about helping with the logistics of physical decline to the far more difficult assessment of mental decline. Her place card was titled: MEMORY CARE. Our guest explained that admission was not based on ability to perform the six living activities, even though help in those areas might be needed. She handed out a brochure that listed eight signs that might indicate dementia was the culprit. They were: DISORIENTED, SELF NEGLECT, ISOLATION, PHYSICAL CHANGES, FAILURE TO MANAGE FINANCES, NEGLECT OF HOME, HOARDING, NOT SAFETY CONSCIOUS.

She explained that seniors with dementia are not good judges of what care they need and someone else has to realize what is going on and have them assessed by their physician. She strongly encouraged those listening on YouTube to be advocates for their parents or grandparents who seem to be declining. She closed with the reassurance that all memory care facilities are secure and focused on safety to keep residents from wandering off.

Her presentation was sobering and the presenter from RESIDENTIAL CARE HOMES helped us make the transition to his topic by claiming, "My mother does very well in the memory care facility we selected. My father, on the other hand, was mentally okay but needed help with his medications and hygiene. We had many wonderful choices between group homes and foster homes, but my wife, Carolyn, and I decided to try another option that I would like to tell you about. Our children are grown and Carolyn works from home while I travel a lot. She felt she would like to take care of Dad, which would give them both company. However, she needs peace and quiet to work while he needs daily monitoring. Our research turned up a fabulous company that met our needs perfectly." At this point he passed out brochures which showed the latest in MEDcottage housing.

"There are a lot of choices for grown children who want their parents close, on the same property, but not in the same house. These pods are one option. They are modular buildings with practical floor plans that can be customized for your parent.

Because we wanted Mom to be able to visit with Dad, we opted for the temporary medical cottage that is actually a kit assembled inside of a two-bay garage. It is beautifully built and equipped with cutting edge technology to allow monitoring from the home and its proximity allows easy visiting and quick response if needed. The added safety feature of the enclosed garage allows us to relax when Mom is visiting because we know she cannot wander off.

"There is a new wave of wheelchair-friendly, innovative solutions to help solve the issues of independent adults needing help. To name a few there are granny flats, elder cottages, tiny houses, and accessory dwellings. With the aging of the baby boomers, these companies are tapping into growing markets to keep seniors close while using technology to assist caregivers.

"These are truly amazing options. I am a convert after seeing how happy Dad is when Mom comes to see him. Without the infrastructure, we could not have handled their needs. I highly recommend downsizing to this option **before** care is needed."

Adrienne muttered brusquely, "Well I don't see how that option is good for someone who is used to living in a mansion." At this point, Carmen was making the rounds passing by her with freshly brewed tea; she gave her sister a scathing glare, which Adrienne ignored.

Turning to our next presenter, I said, "Will you tell us when nursing homes become the best option?" Nodding she began, "Actually our facilities offer residential care until end of life and, in another part of the facility, we offer rehabilitation. So, sometimes placement in the nursing facility is a step along the way to recovery. We offer 24/7 skilled nursing assistance. For someone coming out of the hospital, we might be the best option to get them healed, recovered, and back home or into assisted living."

Gesturing toward the ex-nurse from assisted living she said, "Gretchen here is one of our favorite people to give a needs assessment. Often, she will notice an area where a change in the care plan can increase the quality of life for a resident. She is the one who determines the next step for our seniors who are with us for rehabilitation.

"For our seniors who are with us for the long term, we offer medical and social services from our skilled nurses and caregivers. We meet with a senior's family members to draw up end-of-life agreements whenever possible. If appropriate, we work with the hospice team. However, the skilled nursing environment is heavily regulated and is driven by medical orders. We must have a physician's orders in place; we are essentially the physician's agents. In answer to your question of when nursing care is the best option, I would say when 24/7 care is needed by skilled nurses."

Our final presenter represented the hospice option. She introduced herself as Becky and thanked us for including her in the conversation about care. She said, "I am glad to be sitting next to home care because we often offer our services in the home or a home-like setting. Hospice is a specialized service offered to help patients and their families cope with end-of-life issues. Once the physician approves hospice care, then our team provides an umbrella of support which orients all care toward comfort rather than cure. This is possible because the patient and their family along with their physician have decided to accept that the end is near. Hospice allows the patient to be in control of their care within the bounds of the team's plan."

Sensing that we were at the end of the session, Gretchen asked if she could make one more comment that was off topic. "I wonder how many of my other colleagues who encounter end-of-life situations find that odd things happen."

Becky nodded knowingly. She said, "Yes, and, Gretchen, you and I have talked about this. There is a rarified atmosphere when someone is close to dying. Their minds change and allow all sorts of experiences to come up out of the depths. Our hospice caregivers, especially, talk a lot about these end-of-life experiences where their patients see long dead relatives. In their own pragmatic way, the caregivers will predict when a patient is going to 'cross over' as they say."

Standing, to indicate we were finished, I thanked all of the presenters. Carmen and Adrienne had arrived with their coats and I escorted everyone down the hallway. As we reached the foyer, I could hear Lady Alyce and Minnie arguing loudly. I shooed everyone out as Carmen shot up the stairs to see what was going on.

They were actually shouting at each other. I couldn't believe it, and Carmen looked as shocked as I felt. I joined in her attempts to get Lady Alyce over to the settee but soon gave up and turned my efforts to getting Minnie moving toward the door.

The wind went out of their sails as soon as they saw Oskar enter the room. He calmly said, "You two are acting like children. What is wrong?" Lady Alyce pointed an accusing finger at Minnie and said, "You just want to get rid of me by taking me to assisted living. I'm NOT going anywhere—I'll die in my own bed before I'll let you boss me around, Minerva."

At this point Oskar took both her hands and maneuvered her to sit down. I put my arm around Minnie and guided her to the hallway. As we made our way toward her bedroom, we could hear Lady Alyce shout, "You are worthless without me. I saved you from nothingness by supporting you all these years. NOW you need to take care of me like you promised!"

Minnie was sniffing away tears as we paused before her bedroom door, "I'm going to lie down dear." Seeing the stricken look on my face, she patted my hand

and said, "It's true what she said that I have no one else, but that doesn't mean she owns me. I will be okay—don't worry."

Oskar and I were finishing clean-up in the kitchen and discussing what had happened when Carmen came down to say that all was calm. She said she needed to leave to help Uri get his grandfather to an appointment and would be back in two hours or so. Then she asked, "Do you think it's okay if I leave and Adrienne checks in on Lady Alyce? She's up there now."

I acquiesced and Oskar asked that she text him when she got back home. He said, "A lot has happened to the Yew-Mansion household in a few short days, and I want to keep tabs on where everyone is just to be safe." Away she went with a light step, eager to see her friend.

We dropped back into our musings on the impact of Judy-Ray's loss and agreed that we should cancel all remaining tea parties since we just didn't have the support. I said, "We have four more columns to do. I can write up one from today on housing options. Ricky is already working on posting the video. I was thinking that for our next one, we could invite Aamod back. Remember, he was the panelist who didn't get to present last week. I know the book he is reviewing and it is worth its own column. I could sit down with him for a fireside chat which Ricky could film. We could do that with a minimum of fuss and announce that will be our last interview on YouTube. After that, we would have only two more to fulfill the contract with the newspapers."

Nodding, Oskar asked if I thought Lori and Lee would put up with that since they were advertising on the YouTube videos and they had co-signed with the newspaper. "Who knows?" I answered. "I am already worried about not informing Lori that Judy-Ray is not coming back. I know from the big fight upstairs that Lady Alyce is not going to leave this house willingly. I am really worried about Minnie. I saw her standing in the hallway earlier in the day with a lost look on her face. And who knows how this upset has affected her? I think she wants Lady Al to go to assisted living because she fears she can no longer help take care of her."

As people do, we fell into a far ranging conversation about our lives and our children. It was late by the time we realized the house was awfully quiet. I said, "Good grief, we need to get dinner ready. Judy-Ray would be shaking her head with disapproval." Oskar said, "I'll go up and check to see if they want dinner. It is going to be something from the freezer."

He returned with news. "Adrienne is doing homework in the front parlor within earshot; Carmen is due home in 20 minutes. Lady Alyce does want dinner but does not want to come down and Minnie is still sleeping."

Carmen arrived just as I finished preparing a tray of food and she took it upstairs. I gathered my things, ready to leave for the day. Ricky showed up as I was walking out the front door and said, "I am to walk you home, okay?" Smiling, I took his arm and together we walked the half mile to Ruth's house.

I was tired from the long day and glad to be home. I saw Ruth peeking out the small window anxious for my return. "I should have called you—so sorry." A delicious smell wafted out as she opened the door. We waved goodbye to Ricky.

She took everything from me and said, "Tut, tut. Don't worry about me; you have enough on your mind." She had spent the whole day preparing baked chicken, rice, and green beans for dinner. We cleared a spot on the table which was piled high with mail. "Oh," I exclaimed. "I completely forgot about you and Frances getting the addresses. There is so much mail!" She beamed as she showed me the pages and pages of addresses they had compiled. *Yikes what are we going to do with all of these?*

After dinner, I was exhausted and climbed into the loft bed while she questioned me about the goings on up at the big house. Yawning, I recounted all that had happened. Suddenly, I realized that no one had told the old ladies that Judy-Ray was not coming back. *All hell will break loose then,* I thought. *Minnie is going to push for assisted living for sure. This will tip the scales; Lady Alyce will have to give in.*

In the early hours, a strong wind came up and rocked the tiny house, waking me from an uneasy sleep. *Too much rich food, too late at night,* I thought with a sigh. Knowing that I would not be able to get back to sleep, I carefully climbed down the loft stairs with one hand on the wall and one on the railing. I tiptoed past Ruth's berth-like bed and made it to the bathroom without waking her.

I decided to stay downstairs at the kitchen table and write my column. Ruth and Frances had picked out their favorite question; it was sitting on top of the pile. Written on an attached page were their suggestions, which I adopted whole heartedly.

I might as well get it done now. Who knows what tomorrow will bring, I thought as I pulled out my laptop.

Who should i listen to?

Dear Lady Alyce and Minnie: I have fully recovered from a mild stroke. However, now my children are fighting among themselves over what I should do next. All my life, I raised them to be independent and, by golly, they have scattered all over the USA. Now that I cannot take care of myself at home, they are trying to tell me what to do. One wants me to move close so I can see my grandkids and so she can keep an eye on me, but her life is so very busy we talk on the phone only once a week. My son is single, but he travels all of the time. Besides, I don't want to live as a piece of baggage to their lives. I want my own independence, but I don't know if I will be healthy enough to pull it off. How do I decide which kid to listen to?

—Confused

Dear *Confused*: First of all, whatever you decide to do, do it sooner rather than later. You are in a good position to act on this recent scare you have had. By your own account, you are recovered but may need some help to maintain your independence.

Who knows how many good years you have left? You should put yourself in a position to take advantage of the health you do enjoy by deciding what help you need. Did you know that there are people who can assess your needs and create a plan for you to determine the best setting for you based on your abilities? They will be way more objective than your kids.

Remember that you are still the parent in this situation and you can protect yourself from the infighting by making a good decision and then telling your kids what you have decided to do. No doubt about it, there will be tradeoffs as you choose to be near one or the other. But if you move into a senior community or assisted living near your daughter, then your son can visit since he is the traveler. She has the demands of the kids, so her traveling to see you is less likely. If you are nearby, but not requiring her to help you, then you can see the grandkids and not add to her burden. Whatever you decide, do it while you still can!

CAN THE TEAM ADAPT?
Stage Three—Disability

I t was still dark out but Ruth had seen the glowing light from my laptop and got up to brew a pot of English Breakfast tea. I finished emailing the column to Brad. We were sitting and sipping when a light rapping on the door snapped us out of our companionable reverie. I peeked out to see Ricky. "Oh, oh," I said, "something must be wrong for Oskar to send him for me this early."

"Poor boy," said Ruth, "come in while Maggie gets ready." He was a big presence in that little house, but he managed to slide into the kitchenette booth, taking the seat I had vacated. She eagerly fussed over him, pouring tea and asked if he wanted raisin toast. I kept one ear tuned to their conversation as I pulled on my jeans and zipped up my parka. When I came out of the bathroom, he said, "Oskar said for me to get you. There has been an incident and Doc Satcher needs you to help with Minnie so he can focus on Lady Alyce."

We scurried to the big house while Ricky devoured the buttery toast Ruth had wrapped up for him. He would not tell me any more than bemoan that everything was falling apart. I hugged his arm and said, "Just stick with Oskar; he will know what to do."

The mansion was lit from basement to rooftop. The light pouring out through the many stained glass windows was magical in the foggy morning. Ricky left me at the front steps while he went to report to Oskar. Cautiously, I opened the big door, stepped into the foyer and took an immediate right to head up the stairs. As I was going up, Lady Alyce's physician, Doc Satcher, was coming down. "Oh good, you must be Maggie. I am relieved to see you." He stopped to face me. His dark face was deeply lined, his thin white hair was disheveled, and his shirt was buttoned crookedly. *He must have rushed over here.*

"Carmen called me to come over and calm down Lady Alyce. Evidently, Alyce had gotten up very early this morning to approach Minnie. She found her still in bed—not asleep but dead. Her screams woke the household. It's just a panic attack but serious with her heart condition."

"What! I just saw Minnie last night and she seemed fine." Doc Satcher had descended a few steps and he turned, "Please go stay with her body until the medical examiner gets here. We should not leave her unattended until we find out what happened. Carmen is in with Lady Alyce and I will be back with an injection to sedate her for a while. A home health nurse is coming to help. I will check in with you in a bit."

I stood, frozen in place half way up the stairs. Up above, I could hear Carmen murmuring to Lady Alyce. I could hear the great clock ticking in the hallway below me. We were wrapped in silence when Doc Satcher carefully closed the front door behind him.

I turned and sat down on the step, my head in my hands. "Go sit with her," he had said. *But, I had never even seen a dead person,* I complained to myself. My mind raced back to that awful night when the ambulance had come to the house and medics rushed my husband to the hospital. By the time I arrived, he was in surgery. By the time my sister arrived to wait with me the enormity of what was happening was sinking in. A very tired, young doctor came into the empty waiting room. He approached me with a look on his face that instantly signaled bad news. "I am so sorry to say that we lost your husband."

"Lost him?" I said. "Yes he died on the operating table."

Unbeknownst to me, at the pronouncement of his death the great wheels of the funeral industry began to turn, ferreting him away out the back door and into a windowless van they use to retrieve bodies. He had said he wanted cremation; he had willingly signed the Advanced Directive form years ago in our attorney's office. The next thing I remember in the whirlwind of events is holding a small, very heavy box with his name engraved on the outside.

Lost had been the right word. I was still groping around trying to find my old sense of home. Sobbing from the heat of the memory, I shook myself back to the reality of being on the stairs. Oh, how I dreaded the thought of going into Minnie's room, of sitting beside her. *What was I supposed to do there?*

The phrase, *keep a vigil*, sprang to my mind. I went back down the stairs and gathered up a handful of the tall candles that Judy-Ray kept in the butler's pantry, found some matches, and took the candelabra from the main dining table.

Paraphernalia in hand, I slowly climbed the curving staircase. Peeking into Lady Alyce's bedroom, I saw Carmen sitting beside the bed softly reading out loud. *Ah ha*, I thought and went back down the stairs to the front parlor where I grabbed the nearest book on the small library shelf. Softly, I crept back up the stairs and turned right down the hall where I stopped in front of Minnie's plain bedroom door.

Carefully, I put everything down next to the doorway. I was afraid to actually look at Minnie. My plan was to go in and pull the blanket over her head before I set up the candles and sat down with my book. Softly, I turned the knob and peeked inside. The small room was dark; I could see Minnie's figure lying on the narrow bed, her face a pale sheen in the gloomy light. Creeping forward, I went to pull up the quilt but realized that her arms were folded on top of the blankets. I admonished myself, *No— don't move her.*

Her dresser top was covered with a lacy runner which I slid out from under a hand mirror and hair brush. I oh-so-carefully laid the light filigree material over Minnie's face without really looking at her. I scurried back to the door and stood in the hallway for a bit, listening. Yes, the clock was still ticking and Carmen was still reading. All else was absolutely still.

I gathered my props and set up the candelabra on the dresser top. The match strike flashed light into the room and flared as the first candle caught fire. I lit up all four and settled into a chair opposite the bed under the tall window with book in hand.

As I sat there calming my pounding heart and telling myself to breathe, the minutes ticked by. The old house creaked and the wind rattled the branches against Minnie's window. Feeling calmer, I looked at the book I had clutched in my hands. The title was, *The Creaking of the Tented Sky: The Ticking of Eternity. Poems by Edna St. Vincent Milay.*

Oh, a book of poetry, I thought, *this is just what I need.* My mind went back to what the physics professor had told us about time. He said time was just a measurement of the wear and tear of riding the planet's rotations through space. I imagined myself at the top of the tented sky looking down at the mansion, at Minnie's bedroom, and at myself sitting in that hard backed chair. I could not imagine that the whole thing was moving; it all seemed so very still.

Even though Minnie was old, I simply did not think she would die like this. I remembered that the professor had told us that how long one person would live would depend on their DNA and their life decisions.

I looked at Minnie's shape on the other side of the room. "What choices did you make that ended your ride last night?" I asked out loud, remembering the argument with Lady Alyce. I crossed over to her bedside and asked her covered face, "Did you say that you were going to assisted living with or without her?"

Kneeling, I put my head down on the narrow bed, "You poor thing, she bullied you into staying here with her until you just gave up." I cried then because of my failure to protect her, because of our human failings which hurt each other, because death was so very final. Minnie was gone; she was simply gone from her cold, still body.

How long I knelt there I did not know. When the medical examiner knocked lightly upon entering, I came to my senses and stood up. Oh how my knees hurt! I hobbled to the chair and sat watching as she and her assistant went to Minnie and began their careful examination. Carmen came to lead me away; she said that Doc Satcher had sent a nurse to relieve her and he wanted us downstairs now.

We could hear the clinking of crystal glasses as we approached the dining room. Oskar was there pouring brandy for Doc Satcher. Each of us in turn accepted his offer as Ricky passed out the glasses. "A toast to Minnie," said Oskar and we all chimed in. When the chatter settled, Doc Satcher said, "Soon the funeral home will pick up Minnie's body. The medical examiner will tell us what happened—I suspect she died of heart failure."

Oskar asked if the Doc knew she had heart trouble. "No, I never treated Minnie. I always came for Lady Alyce since she has been my patient for the last 25 years. She is one of four I have left. Since I retired, I only make house calls so I have very few.

"I have called you together to talk about what might happen next since you will be affected by the upcoming changes." I saw Adrienne's face darken and knew that her worst fears were about to come true—she had fought hard against the tide of change. I remembered her telling me when I first met her that she would do anything to stay in school. Now, both her job and her housing were threatened by what was happening.

There were footsteps in the hallway and the medical examiner came in asking Doc Satcher to sign her paperwork. She said to us, "If you want to say goodbye, they are bringing her down the stairs now." We filed out to gather in the foyer, watching as two attendants from the funeral home were maneuvering a stiff canvas bag feet first down the curved staircase and onto the waiting gurney.

I was thankful they had left the top unzipped so that we could say goodbye. They had wrapped the dresser scarf under her chin and tied it on the top of her head. She looked so peaceful that I was no longer afraid. *This is how I will remember her.* Carmen approached the gurney while the attendants stood back. I joined her and soon the others gathered around. Gently brushing back Minnie's gray wispy bangs, Carmen began to recite the Lord's Prayer and we all joined in. After the AMEN, I patted Minnie's cold cheek. I was shocked at how rigid her skin felt. The attendants rolled the gurney out onto the porch before they zipped the bag closed and carried her to a plain-looking, white van.

Carmen and I were crying as we all moved en masse back to the dining room. Doc Satcher was still sitting at the table. The look on his face said he had seen it all before; he was focused on finishing his paperwork. We resumed our seats and Oskar poured another round and looked to Doc, waiting for him to continue. "I have made arrangements for skilled nurses rotating through for the next 48 hours.

Carmen I want you to be available in case there is a gap in coverage. Oskar I want you to take responsibility to lock down the house and keep everyone out of the private areas until Lee can get here and decide what to do. I have ordered meals on wheels which will take care of Lady Alyce and the nurses. I assume the rest of you will manage on your own." With that he got up and stretched. "Oh, my aching back," he complained. "I am on my way and will be back later this afternoon."

We sat stunned by the turn of events.

Adrienne's phone chirp brought us back to our uncertain reality. She texted furiously for a moment, then said, "Lori wants us to meet with her and Lee here tomorrow at noon. She will tell us then what is going to happen. In the meantime, she wants us to keep doing our jobs. Also, we should cancel any scheduled tea parties."

I was surprised, "Boy, that was fast. Doc Satcher must have texted her when we were with Minnie." Turning to Adrienne I asked if she thought he had told her about Judy-Ray as well. "I will do it now," she said and returned to her phone.

Sighing, I said to Oskar "I am going home to bed. I feel like I am fighting a cold— see you tomorrow—I hope." Carmen, Ricky, and Oskar looked at me as if I were deserting them. "Are you guys okay?" Oskar nodded his head and asked if I needed anything. "Just a whole lot of sleep," I said.

I was relieved to get home and let Ruth fuss over me. She insisted that I take a hot bath and lie down on her bed. "I will be right back," she called as she went across the way to Frances' trailer to tell her they were not going to do mail today. When I awoke from my nap, she was eager to talk. "Okay, now tell me all about it," she said as she pulled up her chair next to me and held my hand as I began to tell her of all that had happened.

We gathered at noon the next day. Lori was seated at the foot of the table and Lee at the head. Adrienne had her laptop open to take notes. *She is going to be Lori's new assistant,* I thought as I watched them whisper with their heads close together. Lee was shuffling papers and cleared his throat to signal that the meeting was to start.

Evidently, Doc Satcher had been at the house earlier and had gotten Lady Alyce to sign the guardianship papers. Lee explained, "This means that I am now making the decisions and I will decide what is best for Lady Alyce." His look challenged any opinion to the contrary.

He droned on about the legal implications for the mansion and his fiduciary duty to finally meet the death-bed wishes of his father to turn over everything to the city. "And I mean everything. The city is interested in transforming this old house into a museum and they want all the archival material kept in place until they can bring in their own people to evaluate what is here. In the meantime, Adrienne will act as my agent and inventory everything in the house."

I peeked a glance at her. She was sitting primly taking notes as he spoke as if he wasn't even talking about giving her the lifeline she needed to stay in school. *Good for her*, I thought, *more power to her for landing on her feet.*

Carmen asked what would happen to Lady Alyce. Lee explained that Doc Satcher wanted her in a nursing home for observation and rehabilitation. Even though she was still sedated, she understood what was happening and had agreed to move to the facility tomorrow morning. Carmen asked if she could gather her things to make her more comfortable at the new place. With a curt nod from Lori, Lee agreed.

He resumed, "Tomorrow will be the last day we can allow access to the house. Oskar, the city manager has asked that you stay on to keep maintaining the grounds until their people can put a plan in place, which might take months. You and Ricky can continue to live in the bunk house during that time and Adrienne can stay to maintain the interior. Carmen and Maggie, I am sorry to say that after tomorrow, we will no longer need your services. Lori has prepared severance pay for you. The only other loose end is the columns. I guess we will just have to forget about them."

Coming to my senses, I protested this idea. "Lee, I just submitted the fifth column in the original series of eight. We have three more columns to publish, and I have a suggestion for the next one." I hurried before he could tell me to stop. "May I interview one more person tomorrow in the front parlor? No food service is needed. Ricky has agreed to video tape this one last interview. Once we post it, we can give notice that it is the last one on YouTube. After that we would have only two more to write to complete the contract with the newspapers."

I held my breath waiting for what I was certain would be a no. Surprisingly, Adrienne chimed in with her support. "Lee, this would allow an orderly transition; we don't want the law firm's reputation to be trolled because we quit in the middle of a popular YouTube series. After Maggie writes the next column which will be the last interview posted on line, then we can focus on only the newspapers. For the seventh column, I could help Lori write it; we could make it on Wills and Advance Directives. We can figure out the final column later."

I was proud of her! She truly knew how to jump on an opportunity. The look of frank appraisal on Lee's face showed that he realized he had found a talent. *She may go far with this firm. Lori, you better watch out.*

He harrumphed around for a while mulling it over and finally delegated it to Lori and Adrienne to figure out what to do with the columns. As he and Lori gathered their papers the rest of us sat waiting for the bosses to go.

Adrienne walked them to the front door where they held a second meeting. We could hear them as we hurriedly planned our schedule for the next day. Carmen told us that she had accepted Uri's invitation to come and live at his grandfather's house where they could both help care for him. Her face beamed when she told us her news.

Oskar and Ricky congratulated each other that they did not have to move right away. I hugged them both and told them that I was glad we had a plan. I promised to be back and ready to interview Aamod tomorrow. Ricky said he would get the camera set up. I was greatly relieved that I had already submitted this week's column on time. Our schedule was changing daily, but our newspaper deadline was always Friday.

Adrienne walked back in and sat at the head of the table. I said, "Good job in maneuvering this next column for me. Thank you. Will you please call Aamod and find out if he is willing to come in for an interview at noon tomorrow? He might be available on a Saturday." She immediately texted him on her phone and before I was out the door, she had his acceptance.

My talk with Ruth that night clarified my thinking. I was ready for an interview that focused on the stage of aging called disability—the stage when help is needed with two or more of the six living functions that our first presenter from the home care agency had talked about: eating, bathing, dressing, toileting, transferring, and maintaining continence.

Ruth pointed out that Lady Alyce was now in this stage because of the setback from her grief over Minnie's death and loss of her support in daily maintenance. There had been a cascading effect—her panic attack had resulted in concerns about her heart which had resulted in sedation and the need for skilled nursing care. While she was in the lowest spot, she signed over guardianship and now someone else was making the decisions about what was best for her.

Heading up to the house the next day, I remembered how stressed out I had been on my first day of work when I could hardly push my bicycle up the gravel path. That seemed like a long time ago and yet only three weeks had gone by.

I settled into the wide-bottomed slipper chair that Lady Alyce used to favor. Tears sprang to my eyes when I realized that she was already gone from her beloved home; they had transported her earlier that morning. Carmen said they were gentle and patient, letting her take her time to go through the house to say goodbye. I resolved to go visit her soon.

Aamod arrived, all smiles. Carmen had set up the tea cart for us. She knew he was looking forward to our special Rose Tea. We were seated in front of the exquisitely carved fireplace. It was crowned by a two-foot high arch with a deeply inset stained glass window. One of Lady Alyce's ancestors had commissioned it to memorialize the death of a young man. Three pink and blue flowers surrounded one closed bud symbolic of the parents, sister, and deceased boy.

Ricky was filming from the side to showcase this special window as the backdrop for our interview. Aamod explained that the book he reviewed, *Being Mortal,* had inspired him to switch his major to pre-med. "The author, Atul Gawande, is a son to immigrants who were both physicians. In fact, his father was born in India near my home town. Atul is a surgeon in Boston and a writer on public health. His clinical experience as well as the personal experience of his father's death makes him a highly credible voice on the need to reform our health care system.

"Atul began to question the benefit of surgery on older patients. He realized that the entire system is awash with people who are unprepared to face their own mortality. He argues that physicians are asked to play a role they were not trained for; it is called the dying role and was once universally held by a spiritual consultant, a rabbi, or a priest."

Aamod paused and put his hand on his heart. "My theory is that because many people are without a belief system to help them at life's end and because our modern society holds science as sacred, physicians are placed in the role of ultimate authority. Patients arrive at the hospital in trouble of some sort, scared of what is happening, and just want the doctor to fix it."

He stood up and started to pace back and forth across the worn rug of the parlor. "In my hometown in India, we surround our elders with helpers of all ages who watch out for them and offer care as they can. Here, in America, our seniors become isolated, because independence is highly valued. But what happens when independence is no longer possible?" he asked shrugging his shoulders.

"Atul points out that those who have not had conversations about the inevitability of death and the limits of what doctors can do are doomed to let the default position of the health care system take over. Some are paralyzed with fear and have a fantastical view that the doctor can do a procedure and turn back the clock. This is not the case, especially with a frail patient."

I encouraged Aamod to sit down as his pacing was distracting. He had become more agitated the more he paced. I refreshed his cup and asked if his author gave practical advice using that list of six living activities we had learned about from one of the other panelists.

Stretching out his feet toward the small gas fire burning in the grate, he opened his black notebook and flipped through its pages while answering my question. "Yes, you will remember that the six living activities that our first presenter from the home care agency talked about were eating, bathing, dressing, toileting, transferring, and maintaining continence. To gain a glimpse into his patients' lives, Atul asks eight questions that are precursors to needing help with the six living functions." Finding the passage he was looking for in his book, he said, "Can you shop for yourself, prepare your own food, maintain your housekeeping, do your own laundry, manage your medications, make phone calls, travel on your own, and handle your finances?

"By putting it this way, his patient can imagine their life and easily answer yes or no. Their answers give Atul a baseline which becomes an anchor point in all subsequent conversations. You see he needs to be able to explain the risks and benefits of whatever procedure he is proposing. Using the baseline, he can vividly describe the tradeoffs the patient must accept in order to give informed consent. Giving odds to a patient is abstract. Telling which life activities might be affected as an outcome of the surgery is illuminating. If a patient were to use that mindset they might interpret a diagnosis as directions rather than automatic defeat."

I had written down the eight questions and told Aamod that this was a very helpful tool as was the idea of a baseline. He said, "Remember, aging saps resiliency. Old age is a continuous series of losses which accumulate to the point where we cannot manage on our own. The downward trend toward losing independence is inevitable. Dr. Gawande says it is as inevitable as the sunset.

"Aging is a losing proposition. Medicine can only offer maintenance measures and patch jobs. The aging body is preparing you for death—the final stage of life. At some point you will be glad for the release. Old age is not a diagnosis. Your body must deliver you to death's door.

"The physician's job is to be clear with the patient. The patient's job is to have the courage to face their own mortality so that they can make the best decisions even in the drama and trauma of the hospital. The stakes are very high for a patient because a lost opportunity to prepare can lead to false optimism. The patient who refuses to grapple with the inevitable will fall prey to the tendency of the health care system to invade and that may leave them accepting risks that are too high. The unintended consequences of an invasive procedure may leave them in the exact opposite situation they want. For example, the decision to operate on a fragile patient with heart disease may solve the initial problem but may result in a cascading effect on other systems. At each point of failure, risk versus benefit must again be weighed."

We sat in companionable silence for a minute until a cough from Ricky reminded me that we were filming for our final YouTube broadcast. Rousing myself, I asked, "Did he offer any other helpful decision tools that you can pass on?"

Aamod pursed his lips as he flipped through his little notebook. "Yes," he answered. Here are four very important questions a physician should ask after explaining the risks of a procedure: Do you understand your prognosis? What are your fears about what is to come? What are your goals as time runs out? What tradeoffs are you willing to make? Listening for feedback will ensure that the patient has clearly heard and understands. You can see that coupled with the baseline of the living activities, the physician can address each answer as it relates to what quality of life issues the patient values most."

I was listening closely to him. He was very good at summarizing important information and creating a sort of thumbnail sketch. *He is going to make a good physician because he can explain complex information in a simple way.* I nodded my agreement and said, "Yes, I can immediately relate to how helpful that is. Knowing what you are agreeing to is crucial to weighing the risks. We have to have courage to confront the implications of the procedure. And we have to have courage to face our fears and embrace a new baseline as we come out from under the operation."

Aamod nodded vigorously. "We might die. We might not wake up. That, too, has to be accepted before we give consent. If we want to meet the end of our life on our own terms, then the procedure's risks might not be worth it. It might be better to say 'no thanks' and live with the consequences of the disease. If the risk is to lose the option of ending our life outside of the hospital, then we have to say no. We have to say, I would rather embrace this situation that is killing me than be caught in the vicious cycle of one procedure after another."

Consulting his notebook again, Aamod said, "One last pearl of wisdom from Dr. Gawande that I would give our listeners is this quotation, 'At least two kinds of courage are required in aging and sickness. The first is the courage to confront the reality of mortality…the second kind of courage is the courage to act on the truth we find.' You can see that the good doctor is trying to get out the word that patients need to be prepared for what they might face." With that he closed his notebook and snapped a rubber band around it. I heard Ricky click off the camera.

I thanked Aamod for his time and willingness to come. He joked that he owed us because we had already given him a free lunch and asked, "How is the lady who fell?" At that moment, I realized I had completely put Judy-Ray out of my mind. The blank look on my face triggered Ricky to chime in as he broke down his equipment, "She is doing much better and plans to take Lady Alyce to Minnie's funeral next Tuesday." I gave him a thumbs-up for his smooth rescue.

Just as he was leaving, Aamod reached into his jacket pocket and pulled out a small waxed-paper package. "This is for you Miss Maggie. This is a special scarf that we use in my village to cover the face of a deceased person during the cleansing ritual." Taking it from him, I immediately thought of my clumsy efforts to find something to cover Minnie's face. "Thank you," I whispered. I watched him leave through the glass pane in the front door. *He is going to make a difference in health care,* I thought with a flash of optimism.

Moments later, Adrienne arrived at my side as I was reaching to pull open the big front door. She handed me an envelope and said, "Here is your final paycheck and severance. Lee wanted me to let you know how much he appreciates all that you have done during this important transition."

Smiling my acceptance, I made my pitch. "Listen, Adrienne, we have a little bit of wiggle room, because we have six days before the deadline to post this column from my interview with Aamod. I am going to send it to Brad as soon as I can and let him coordinate it with Ricky's video. In the meantime, you and Lori have almost two weeks to write your column which could focus on the importance of having legal papers in place.

"I just learned that Minnie's funeral is in three days—next Tuesday. I volunteer to put an obituary in the newspaper today to announce the date and time of her memorial service. I think we will get a lot of mail about Minnie's death. I could write the final column with a focus on letters asking about the meaning of life and funeral planning."

She nodded her agreement and gave me a final quick hug. When I reached the bottom of the stairs, I took one long look back at the big Victorian mansion, one final glance at the picturesque setting, reminiscing on all that had happened over the past weeks. I knew I would not be back to this beautiful place.

As I trudged down the gravel path, I realized that I had enjoyed working in this richly appointed world centered on Lady Alyce and her ancestral home. *Yes, I thought, I will stay connected with the girls and perhaps with Oskar.* But I was happy to be heading back to Ruth's humble world centered in her tiny house and her loving community at the trailer park. As I briskly walked the half mile home, I had a sense of reaching an inflection point in my own life's journey. I knew that my time with Ruth would be coming to an end and I would need to pursue my own next steps.

WHO SPEAKS FOR ME?

Dear Lady Alyce and Minnie: My wife passed away a few months ago. I was her caretaker until the end of her life. Because she was less and less able to understand what the doctor was saying, I became her surrogate and made all of the decisions. At one crucial juncture, I told the doctor we would not proceed with the chemotherapy that he recommended (it was the third new medicine). I could not bear to see my dear wife in such pain as she fought against the cancer. I saw a YouTube video about a woman who said she and her husband had to accept that they had run out of hope. They had to switch from a fight mode to an acceptance mode. I took that as guidance and I made the same sort of decision, stopped treatment, and took her out of the hospital. My wife died at home with hospice help and with friends and family nearby. But I miss her so much! How can I bear this suffering of living without her? And how can I bear to put the burden of decision maker on any of my children to speak for me in the future now that I know what it means

—Grieving and Too Much To Ask

Dear *Grieving:* Please accept our condolences on the loss of your wife. We wonder if you would consider a different perspective. You are suffering now because you miss her, not because you think you made the wrong decision, correct? Well, if the tables were turned and she outlived you, perhaps life would have been a terrible burden for her. The grief you feel is right and just given the closeness of your relationship. However, your heroic efforts and decisions have saved her from ending up in a situation that she was mentally unable to handle. You can transform the suffering you are feeling by realizing that you are carrying the heavy load by outliving her.

As far as protecting your children from having to bear the burden of surrogate decision maker, we urge you to consider that you have set a model for them in how you took care of your wife. If you do everything you can now to care for yourself, put yourself into a living situation that gives support where you need it, and make your wishes known you will lessen the burden on the one who volunteers to step into this role. You have learned a lot by going through this journey with your wife, so you can anticipate what might come up. In advance, you can leave written instructions of your wishes so that your surrogate will have your guidance even when you are not able to speak for yourself. It will be your gift of wisdom that keeps on giving.

Legal and Spiritual Protection: *Stage Four—Failing Health*

Alight hesitant rapping on the door woke me. Ruth and I had both slept in, missing our usual Sunday morning trip to church services. Frances used her key to enter saying, "I was getting worried about you two. I thought there might be a gas leak and you were both dead."

"Oh Frannie, come in, come in and start the tea," called Ruth as she began the slow process of getting herself up and going. I stayed in my loft bed luxuriating in knowing that I did not have to go back to work at the mansion. I listened to the two old ladies bantering with each other as I looked out my side window bordering the creek. The tree leaves were shimmering in the light and birds were chirping, swooping, and diving as the sun hatched the bugs they loved.

I leaned over the edge of the loft and took the steaming mug of tea that Frances handed up. She smiled and said, "We are so glad you are coming to the big meeting. We need your professional opinion." My quizzical look cued her into the fact that Ruth had not mentioned this meeting. "Oh, oh, I better let her tell you about it I guess. Now that I know you're okay, I'll go do my shopping. Do you need anything?"

Ruth handed her a list and hustled her out as I sidled past their whispered conversation at the door and made my way to the bathroom. *On to the next thing,* I thought, as I slipped into my seat at the kitchen table eager to hear what Ruth had to say.

"Now listen Maggie, I know that you have already interrupted your life to help me for longer than either of us planned. You know I am very grateful; I could not have made it through without you." She brushed off my dismissals. "I need you to stay just a bit longer because we oldsters have started something that I want you to know about.

"In a week we are having a meeting to formalize our homeowner's association. Our attorney will be here and so will the head guy from St. Vincent de Paul. There are ten units in this manufactured home park and all of us owners have agreed to put the land into trust which St. Vinny's will hold. In exchange they will provide maintenance help for us."

She was very intent on telling me the plans—I nodded to show my interest. "Okay, I am following you. Why do you want to do this?" She had expected this question. "We are all old and we know that we will need help as we get older. So we have made a pact to help each other. This is where the homeowner's association comes in. We use the legal protection provided by the HOA—our name is the Cloud of Witnesses after a verse in scripture. We watch out for each other and we have pledged that as one falls ill, the others will step up to take over care.

"When I first moved here a year ago, we had a resident, her name was Beulah, who knew she was dying. She had refused care and gotten a hospice nurse. One Sunday, she gathered us together to say that she planned to donate her house and space to St. Vinny's when she died. She challenged us to join together to create a homeowner's association as legal protection against our relatives whom she feared would swoop in at the end. She wasn't afraid of suffering at home, but was fiercely afraid of being trapped in the intensive care unit and dying in the hospital.

"She told us that if we wanted to die at home, we were going to have to put legal safeguards in place to prevent our relatives from taking over. Her greatest fear was that her children, who never came to see her, would hear she was failing and would try to intervene. She said that only other oldsters had the wisdom to know when to die.

"So she bequeathed land and money for the common area building and passed on her trailer and her estate as a seed to grow a new community with a good legal foundation. She believed that once we were safe from the outside world, only then could we nurture what she called spiritual security. Over the year, she wrote a guide for us to know what to do for her death. It is called Beulah's Playbook and, with our input, she incorporated rituals and ceremonies from different belief systems—they were practices developed from ancient times to help those whom death leaves behind. We got to try these out for the first time when she died just two weeks before my surgery. She is our true founder. Now, we are living out her dream."

"Oh Ruth," I exclaimed, "that is an amazing project and must bring you a lot of comfort knowing that you have people around you to call on." She nodded emphatically, "Yes, we have been meeting with our attorney to draw up advance directives. We have a buddy system that partners each unit with one other unit, putting us on call to each other. That's why Frances came over this morning. She watches out for me." With a crooked little smile, she added "You too!"

I asked, "What happens to your home after you die?" Smugly, she answered "We have thought of everything. The land is held in trust, but each unit is owned individually giving us the comfort of ownership. As a home becomes available, a new owner is screened by St. Vinny's and brought to us for a vote. That new oldster has to accept their role as one of the witnesses and promise to pitch in. That way we can keep our homeowner's association going and grow our community one to two people at a time. As our founding group ages and begins to die off, we will be replaced by others who are following our scheme to care for each other."

"Bravo! What a fantastic way to face the end of life and find friends to walk that last mile with you. I am impressed!" She clasped my hands across the table, a look of pure pride on her face. *Oh she is so terribly thin,* I thought as I patted her arm.

Ruth agreed to attend Minnie's funeral with me and I promised her I would stay for the meeting scheduled a week from Monday. I told her after that I really must go. My mind turned toward my own decisions yet to be made about where I was heading.

I had been hearing from Ursla about the new neighbors who had purchased my house. They had young children and she was already their "second grandmother." The kitties were fine and one had adopted her invalid husband's lap as her favorite napping spot. My sister was emailing me with plans for a trip to Scotland and wanted me to accompany her.

Dreaming of that trip became my favorite pastime as I whiled away the days helping Ruth sort through her possessions. She had found my book titled, *The Gentle Art of Swedish Death Cleaning* and decided she should try to prepare her tiny home for the person who would come after her. My protests did not faze her. She said over and over, "I don't want you to have to spend any more time dealing with me and my stuff. You have already done enough and I can do it now a few hours at a time."

At one end of the manufactured home park was the Community Center where meetings and meals were held. In this big, open modular building was a common laundry facility, roomy storage cabinets, individual cubbies with locks on them, and a large conference table which could be folded up to make room for special events. Depending on who the social director was for the month, all sorts of activities went on in that plain building.

Frances pushed Ruth in the wheelchair down the smooth cement paths and I pulled the community wagon-barrow to haul her extra clothing and utensils up to the drop box at the Community Center. There, working on the entrance, were two fellows hired to place a sign over the front door that read *SWING LOW-SWEET CHARIOT.* I laughed to see such unabashed acceptance at what life's end can bring.

As we straightened up the common area, Frances told me that she belonged to the choir and they were practicing call-and-response songs for funeral ceremonies.

"Amazing, you guys are really embracing this new idea, aren't you?" She clapped her hands with delight, "Yes, we might even hire ourselves out to sing at funerals. Our name is *Band of Angels* and we just found out that one of our members plays a violin, so we can perform either with a fiddle or a cappella."

Ruth and I took time out of our cleaning routine to pay our respects to Minnie. On Tuesday, we took a taxi to the funeral home only a few miles from the mansion. It was situated next to the old cemetery and was founded the same year construction began on the big house back in the 1890s. Almost all of Lady Alyce's ancestors were buried there. Oskar had told me that one of the promises Minnie extracted when she agreed to be Lady Alyce's companion was that they would make arrangements for her burial in the old cemetery. He said that the agreement provided a gravesite for Minnie that was near the family's tomb. From time to time, she would mention to him how comforting it was to know that she was heading for the old family plot and not the potter's field.

I could not believe that only six days had passed since I sat with Minnie's body in the upstairs room. Carmen was waiting for us by the curb with a wheelchair for Ruth. Our quick introductions were made on the fly as we sped toward the front entrance where Adrienne held the door open.

We rolled into the quiet, deeply carpeted hallway and saw Judy-Ray and her daughters gathered outside of a doorway with a beautiful white wreath on an easel. Peeking into the room, we saw Lady Alyce sitting in a wheelchair near a big, ornamental casket. Oskar stood off to the side waiting respectfully. As soon as he saw us, he wheeled Lady Alyce to the front pew, carefully parked her there, and made his way down the aisle toward us. Whispering for me to wait, he took control of the chair and wheeled Ruth to the front next to Lady Alyce.

He came back ready to usher me to the first pew where Adrienne was sitting. He squeezed my arm as we waited for Judy-Ray to hobble forward. "I am pleased to see you Maggie." I squeezed him back. He leaned close and whispered, "Lady Alyce is just beside herself with guilt. She tells everybody that she killed Minnie by refusing to budge about assisted living. She wails that Minnie must have hated her for it."

I had often wondered about that last, upsetting scene between them and anticipated this response of guilt from Lady Alyce. I had developed a plan that might help. After the mercifully short service which was led by a pastor who did not know Minnie but told us that she was in God's care now, we filed out to the reception room where soft music played in the background. I approached Lady Alyce and knelt down beside her. I was shocked at how much she had aged since I had last seen her on the evening of the fight. She was on a downhill slide that I knew would not be reversed.

I took her hand and she looked at me quizzically. "Lady Alyce I have something for you." I pressed into her trembling hands the small book of poetry I had taken from the front room that morning when Doc Satcher told me to go sit with Minnie. Her blank look told me she didn't understand what I said. I opened the book and pulled out a small piece of faded paper. "Look, here is a note to you from Minnie that was tucked inside of this book of poetry."

Her curiosity brought her into focus and she turned over the small book to see the title. "Oh this was Minnie's very favorite. She used to read to me from it." The tears came then. Carmen was hovering nearby and brought a tissue to wipe her wet cheeks. Arranging Lady Alyce's wooly pink shawl, she asked, "What do you have there?" Extracting the small slip of paper from her freckled hand, she leaned down close to read the note to her out loud. "Dear Al, remember that whatever happens, I love you and will love you forever. Minnie."

With a look of pure joy, Lady Alyce grabbed the paper from Carmen's hand and clasped it to her breast. Sobbing, she said, "She loved me! She really loved me!" Nodding her head over and over, she declared, "Now I can die in peace."

I gave Carmen a smile and wheeled Ruth out to our waiting taxi. She turned her head and called out over her shoulder, "Did Minnie really give you that book?" I kept rolling out into the sunshine, away from the dark, cave-like atmosphere of the funeral home before I answered. As we waited for the driver to help us, I leaned over and whispered into her ear, "Yes, in a roundabout way, Minnie really did give me that book."

In the days after our big outing to the funeral, Ruth began staying in bed—only getting up to make trips to the bathroom. I put in a call to Claire, the hospice nurse, for her to make a visit earlier than her usual weekly check in. She had been assigned to Ruth's case ever since the surgery which was done to relieve a bowel obstruction but without hope that it would do anything other than make tolerable the effects of the colon cancer.

From the moment I met Claire I knew that she was truly called to this profession because her manner was so gentle and reassuring. She spent time taking vitals and listening carefully to Ruth's heart. She nodded when I said that she was sleeping a lot. But when I told her that she had been having dreams, she stopped what she was doing. "Did she tell you about them? Did she say that she saw family who had already passed on?" When I nodded she seemed validated. "It won't be long now; I would say no more than a week to ten days."

I walked with Claire as she stopped to talk with Frances on her way out of the park. Because Frances was on call as my backup, Claire admonished both of us, "Do NOT call 911 or Ruth will be taken to the ER and she does not want that." Writing down her number, Claire stressed that we should call her for any emergency at any time. We reassured her that we knew the drill. Leaving, she said, "I will give her more pain medication if she is suffering, so call me as soon as you suspect she is in trouble. I can be here in ten minutes."

Frances brought over the stacks of mail which kept on coming in response to the advice columns. To make it easy, we had rerouted the mail from the PO Box to her address in the trailer park. We kept Ruth company by sorting the mail and chatting as she slept. Unbeknownst to me, the old ladies had started a pen pal club. When I heard about it, I thought, *Good thing Lee doesn't know anything about this. I'm sure there is some sort of liability lurking for using the information in an unauthorized way.*

Frances explained that the club had six members from the homeowner's association. She and Ruth were supposed to be the organizers; the others were the actual writers. Ruth had become too inactive to help, so the job of opening and sorting the mail had fallen to Frances. She had four piles in separate boxes. She sighed as she explained that one pile was for shredding. They were crank letters that she needed to screen from the eyes of her writers. I wondered aloud why some people would take the time to pass on hatred like that. She said, "I think they are very afraid of dying. They push it away as hard and as far as they can because it can be so very frightening if you really think about it." I asked, "Are you afraid of dying?"

She looked at me with her big, kind eyes, "Not anymore. Not since I have found this group of wonderful people here who will help me as I need it. Once a week, there is a yoga class offered in the Community Center by a young Buddhist monk. For people who want to face their fear of death, he teaches us to visualize our own ideal death scene. He says we have to imagine the landscape surrounding our exit from this world and visualize ourselves in it ahead of time. If we practice breathing and focus on our scene, hearing the sounds and seeing the colors all the while breathing deeply, then that will help us when we are actually on our deathbed."

She giggled and coyly said, "He is really cute too!" Ruth whispered "amen" from her bed where she had been watching and listening. We continued with the mail; the second pile was called "welfare check" and was given to St. Vinny's for them to follow up with; the third pile was "no answer needed;" and the fourth one was to pass onto the pen pal writers for a response.

Together, we hauled everything up to the Community Center for distribution. The good mail was distributed to the correct cubbies and we took the trash out the back door. There was a chain link fence behind the building with a side gate to an enclosed area where the trash bins were kept. One was a secure container and we piled everything in there that was to be shredded. Next to the area was Beulah's former trailer which had been designated for the caretaker that St. Vinny's placed on site. Frances told me that in exchange for housing, his task was to fix small problems for the residents and provide 24/7 security. She said that his name was Clay and he had been homeless before he came to them. "Everyone just loves him and he feels proud that we chose him. He is very protective of us. We call him Papa Bear." Pulling the wagon beside her, I thought, *You deserve to feel safe—a papa bear is just the ticket.*

The day of the big meeting came. Ruth insisted on going; she was excited with their success and wanted to participate even though it was all she could manage. I told her I was impressed with the efficiency of their attorney. She said they picked a "real young one" so that he would be around for a while. The signing ceremony was followed by a potluck. Everyone stayed except for the attorney who rushed off to his next appointment.

Papa Bear Clay was making the rounds, socializing with everyone before he left with the representative from St. Vinny's to show off the new perimeter security system he had installed. I was pressed into making a short speech and praised them all for their innovative solutions to the very difficult problems that end-of-life can present. "You know you are a model for others." They nodded and clapped. "You know you have taken control over how you want to die." They nodded and clapped and threw in a couple of AMENs. Getting into the spirit of the call-and-response, I said, "You know that you are claiming power for ALL old people by showing them a new way." At this they broke out stamping their feet and clapping. I called out "AMEN" and they all cheered. It was a huge success.

The next few days passed lazily. Ruth slept deeply and was seldom awake; the meeting had completely fatigued her. Claire began to stop by every day to check on her. She started using an opiate patch to help ease Ruth's pain and inserted a catheter so she did not have to struggle to the bathroom. Frances stepped up as nurse assistant and kept Ruth clean and comfortable.

One by one, the neighbors dropped in to visit and hold her hand as she drowsed. She was intermittently conscious. At one point, Ruth opened her eyes as Claire was listening to her heart. She asked, "Is this the end?" Claire answered, "You will know when it is." Ruth protested, "But I never died before, I don't know what to do at the end." Claire whispered, "Go with the flow."

Saturday was sunny. Ruth had rallied a bit and seemed better. In a burst of optimism I had prepared her favorite recipe for meat loaf which was baking with potatoes in the tiny oven. Even though I knew she would not be able to eat, at least the house was filled with a delicious smell. With a glass of wine in hand, I stepped out on the back porch which was positioned to overlook the small hill leading down to the creek. This space was one of my favorites, especially when the sun was shining. I had picked up the daily newspaper and was looking forward to catching up with the outside world as I knew that I would soon be leaving this special place and finding my own way forward.

I thought back to what Frances had said about imagining the landscape of your death. With eyes closed and my face turned to the sun, I thought, *Yeah— this moment right now will do.* I absorbed the sound of the birds calling to each other, the far away music of the creek, the soft voice of Frances singing to Ruth, the faint sounds of traffic beyond the trailer park. It was a perfect scenario that I locked in my mind for future recall.

As life does, that perfect scene changed with a chill setting in. I pulled a blanket over my lap and snapped open the paper searching for Lori and Adrienne's column.

Legal protections for end-of-life
www.aging.com

To the fans of Lady Alyce and Minnie: We regret to inform you that Minerva Lucille Barclay (Minnie) passed away in her sleep. We offer the following information to help those of you who have written asking how to create a comprehensive strategy for safeguarding one's health, property and finances. **Note: This is the second to last column in this newspaper series.**

Will: A last will and testament indicates how a person's assets will be distributed among beneficiaries after they pass away. The writer of the will (known as the testator) can also specify a person (the executor) to manage the probate process and distribution of the estate. A will does not take effect until the testator dies. (*A will should be opened soon enough to guide relevant decisions.*)

Advance Directives: Advance directives are written instructions for future medical care in case you are unable to make or communicate decisions (for example, if you are unconscious or mentally incapacitated). These are also called healthcare directives. There are a few different forms and documents that can be used to articulate healthcare preferences. (**Only** *those completed by a physician constitute orders. All medical personnel* **MUST** *have physician orders to vary from standard protocol.*)

Living Will: Unlike a traditional will explained above, a living will provides instructions for use while the testator is still alive. A living will goes into effect when the testator is no longer able to communicate their wishes for health care or is not competent to make such decisions. This document is a type of advance directive that describes how a person wants <u>emergency and/or end-of-life care</u> to be managed.

Do Not Resuscitate (DNR) Order: A DNR form is completed by a physician or health care provider stipulating that a patient does not wish to receive life-prolonging treatment if cardiac or respiratory arrest occur. These procedures include CPR, intubation, and use of a ventilator, defibrillation and other related methods of resuscitation. (*Patients should wear a DNR bracelet to alert medical personnel.*)

Physician Orders for Life-Sustaining Treatment (POLST): Some states have replaced or supplemented DNR orders with POLST forms. They are very similar but POLST forms go into further detail regarding specific treatments like antibiotics and feeding tubes. Like DNR orders, POLST forms are intended to be a condensed version of your living will that medical professionals can quickly and easily consult when deciding on a plan of care. (**NOTE:** A POLST is needed to turn an Advanced Directive into medical orders that medical personnel will follow. Some states have a POLST registry.)

Powers of Attorney: Power of attorney (POA) documents allow a person (the principal) to give a trusted individual (the agent) the ability to make decisions on their behalf. A POA can be written to grant an agent the ability to act in very broad terms or to only take specific actions. This document can also be customized to take effect upon its creation (durable POA) or upon the principal's incapacitation (springing POA). If a person becomes incapacitated without drawing up POA documents, their family members may have to go through the long and expensive process of seeking guardianship to be able to manage their affairs.

THE LANDSCAPE OF DEATH:
Stage Five — Active Dying

I was disappointed in the minimum effort put into the column. The day before it was due, Adrienne had called me in a panic, wanting to know if I could write it for her. She was overwhelmed with work and school. I told her no—I could not with such short notice. As a stop gap, I suggested that she just use the law firm's standard definitions for end-of-life issues. I reassured her that I would write and submit the final column of the series to complete the syndication contract. She said that Lee was counting on the income to help with Lady Alyce's care.

In our quick chat, I found out that Lady Alyce had stopped fighting to go back home. Carmen had volunteered to continue visiting her and she was able to smooth the transition. Once Lee had guardianship, he had moved quickly to turn over the mansion; the city had already sent over staff to begin the transition. They had optimistic plans to refurbish it as a showplace since it was one of the great houses built at the inception of establishing the city.

As I sat in the sunshine punctuated by white puffy clouds, I was thinking about my upcoming last column. When Ruth had rallied earlier in the day, she and Frances had agreed on one particular letter as the centerpiece of the final advice column. I was struggling with the question of whose name to put on it since Minnie was gone and Lady Alyce was far removed from writing it. In the end, I decided to stay with our format.

I heard a knock at the front door and called out, "I'm back here. Come on back." Two home health aides had arrived to give Ruth a sponge bath and other comfort care. "Go on in and call me if you need anything," I told them as I stretched out, savoring the chance to finish reading the paper and to rest in anticipation of a long night.

The aides came to tell me they were leaving; I thanked them and waved goodbye as they walked down the path toward the small parking lot at the end of the compound. Frances shouted out to me while I was still standing on the porch. "Claire called to say that she will be here soon. She wants me to relieve you at midnight tonight." I nodded my understanding and went inside.

Ruth seemed to be resting peacefully but was making a low sound that was otherworldly. I checked her pulse which was slow and thready. She had fallen into inaction so quickly after her earlier revival that I was worried. As I waited for Claire, I set the table for only two, knowing that Ruth would not be eating with us; she had refused even liquids for two days now. I hoped that the familiar smell of food in the oven would be a meager comfort to her.

Claire arrived. One look at me and she knew I was anxious about keeping watch. She patted my arm and said, "I see you have dinner for us—thank you—that will be a great help as I need to leave here to check on another patient." At my look of concern, she said, "Maggie, you will be fine—just follow Ruth's lead. She is not in pain, she is just passing over the threshold and you are here to hold her hand."

I nodded, tears streaming down my face. "Come on," she said, "you serve while I check on her; then we will eat whatever it is that smells so delicious."

Finishing with Ruth, Claire slid into her seat at the kitchenette-booth and asked me for an update. I explained that Ruth was making odd sounds. Claire said, "This sort of keening or moaning is not uncommon when a person is close to dying. It is her final goodbye. Did you notice that her breath is becoming irregular?"

"Yes, I was sitting by her and waiting for her to start breathing again after a minute or so of a spell of halting breath then she gasped and started up again. The tempo of her breathing had changed from regular to uncertain. What does that mean?"

"It means that Ruth is having a peaceful death. I have seen many variations, but the older a person is then typically the crossing over is less dramatic. Someone who is struggling to live is actually fighting death. Life and death are locked in a battle. Death wants the body. Life is not ready to stop using it yet.

"Our job as hospice nurses is to keep our patients as comfortable as possible. One of the great benefits of hospice is we can give patients control over their treatment as much as possible within the confines of the hospice team's goals. For example, if a hospice patient does not want to follow hospice care orders for rehabilitation, we don't push them. If they want more morphine, we allow it, within reason, because we believe they are the best judge of their pain. We provide a sanctuary space between the nursing home and death. People call us in to gain protection to die at their own pace, often at home, without invasive procedures or being taken to the ER if they fall. Once hospice is authorized, we step in to help both the patient and their family members. What we find is that because our society hides dying people away in institutions, our families are seldom exposed to end-of-life reality. They don't know what to do so they default to calling 911."

I flashed back to my own end-of-life encounter with 911 when I called them to help my husband. "But don't we need to try to do everything? Shouldn't we call for help?" I asked.

"Of course you should if you are calling for someone who is not under doctors' orders. The ambulance will take them into the ER and they will get into the system and the wheels will be set in motion and all the amazing resources of the hospital will be brought to bear.

"I'm talking about that one aspect of the health care system that is focused on the patient who is not expected to get better, who cannot or does not want to withstand the recommended medical treatment, or has no other options for curative treatment. I am talking about people who are dropping from one baseline down to another without hope of recovering from progressive failures. At some point you have to switch from fighting to acceptance. That is when hospice is the appropriate combination of skilled nursing and of comfort care."

"Claire, what should I do if Ruth passes away when you are gone?" She smiled in a kindly way and said, "Maggie, all you have to do is be present. We are only trying to help Ruth make the transition as she has said she wants it to occur. She is ready for her ending. You can see that it is happening already, all she needs from us is to be with her, to hold her hand in the silence beyond words."

Nodding acknowledgement of her explanation, I said "I know this is a stupid question, but I have heard stories that hospice workers tell of their patients seeing ghosts." She laughed and said, "I know. Every hospice worker has a story to relate. I believe that is because of a momentary merging of two worlds that occurs at death and strange things can happen at that intersection. Stories tell of all sorts of phenomena. I have heard stories that clocks stop at the instant of death, lights appear, the room fills with smoke, and patients who are dying see people in their room."

"Do you mean like those stories of a white light and a long tunnel?" She shook her head, "No, those are near death experiences. That is when a person is injured or in surgery and they report an out-of-body event. There are many studies of near death experiences because they have universal qualities to them and the patient is alive to talk about it and continues to live with their reported experience. I think they are very interesting.

"But, we're talking about non-traumatic circumstances where a patient quite calmly will describe seeing their deceased parent, for example. When hospice workers hear that, then we know we are nearing the end of life passage. Whether or not there is a scientific explanation for what the patient sees is irrelevant to us; only our authentic acceptance of the patient's reality is important.

"You will be fine," Claire said as she prepared to go on her way.

A deep quiet descended as I cleaned up the kitchen and lit the candle I had purchased especially for this evening. It was scented with evergreen which I knew Ruth loved. I put it in the middle of the stovetop because she was so fastidious about open fire. The other candles were battery powered; I placed them on the table and by her bedside. Then, I brought out a bottle of brandy and set out two glasses; I poured one for me and left the bottle sitting next to the other glass for any unexpected guest.

Contented with my day and our conversation, I sat next to Ruth and held her hand in mine. Her hand was cool and comforting. I had wrapped myself in an afghan that she had knitted and I was sitting in her favorite chair. I began to read out loud to her.

Ruth could feel the warmth of Maggie's hand and the soft tone of her voice. She let her mind float as she listened to the rising and falling of Maggie's words. It seemed to her that she was a leaf that had let go of its link to the tree of life. And she floated down in a wide gentle spiral—down—down; and as she swirled in the currents of her mind, her loved ones came from the recesses to float with her. There was her mother—Oh God—there her father and drifting past was her dear daughter who had died as a young woman. Maggie's voice droned on and Ruth's mind drifted until beneath her falling was a figure who rolled over to face her. She gasped to see her beloved husband who had died so horribly, now restored to the young man she had loved at first sight. He held out his arms to her and when he smiled, Ruth's heart burst and she fell into one bright instant of transition from the life she loved so much.

I felt her go and grasped her hands, crying out "Ruth, oh Ruth."

How long I sat there I could not say, but I realized that Frances had come in. Crying softly, she folded Ruth's hands over her heart and urged me to move to the table. I took the Hindu scarf that Aamod had given me and unfurled it to cover Ruth's face.

Frances and I drank a brandy, cried, told stories, cried some more, and toasted Ruth's passing. Looking around the small home, I noticed that the candle had gone out. "Did you blow out the candle, Frances?" "Not me," she said. Shaking off my eerie feeling, I said, "Oh, I guess now I have my own hospice story to tell."

Frances had called the two community members whose turn it was to serve as death doulas. They had been trained to step in and care for the deceased body on behalf of the community. Beulah's Playbook called them midwives to death and spelled out the steps they would take to begin the ritual process of washing Ruth and preparing her for burial. Their presence signaled that my role was over.

Frances said, "Come on now, it's time for you to rest. I will take care of her from here." Gratefully, I climbed the small staircase to my loft bed and fell instantly asleep.

The sound of running water roused me; I peered over the edge to see two women methodically uncovering Ruth's body in the bed below me. The designers of the tiny house had thought of everything to make the house user friendly. The lower bunk of the loft bed pulled out completely into the living area. It was on industry strength roller bars, sliding out smoothly and clicking into its locking mechanism. This allowed easy access to move around the bed and tend to Ruth.

One of the women, Emily, saw me watching and put her finger to her lips to signal the sacred intimacy of their washing ceremony. I noticed they had relit the candle along with several sticks of incense. Classical music played in the background. The scene from my perch was magical and seemed sacred in its purposeful attention to Ruth's body as a beautiful vessel.

I realized that I was watching at-home funeral preparations. They rolled her on one side to remove the heavy duty towels and the long vibrating pad that Claire had started using to fend off bedsores. Efficiently they replaced all the linen with new absorbent towels.

Moving in unison, they sponge bathed Ruth from toes to head. Emily explained later that they had to work swiftly to stay ahead of increasing rigor. After the washing ceremony, they dressed her in a long, flannel nightgown that had been split down the back. The colorful Hindu scarf that I had put over Ruth's face was now folded up like a bandana, tucked under her chin, and knotted on the top of her head.

I would learn later that this practice was to keep her mouth closed as her jaw muscles relaxed in death. The doulas had placed two silver-dollar sized stones on her eyes. Each stone was painted with a colorful mandala. *Such a charming effect,* I thought, *really very nice.* They began to wrap her in a shroud that had been made by the community especially for Ruth. It was a work of art covered with embroidered designs made of brightly colored threads and beads.

They began by pulling it under her, hem side up, as if they were changing a bed sheet with the patient still in bed. *Quite an art,* I thought as I watched from on high. Once they had centered Ruth on the shroud-covered bed, they folded it up over her feet, then pulled it diagonally over one side and tucked her in; repeating the process on the other side. Soon she was wrapped like a baby in a swaddling blanket with her face framed by the top of the shroud. This way she was ready for the viewing to take place in the morning at the Community Center.

The next steps as laid out in the Playbook directed them to place Ruth's body on the shroud board which was a special hemlock panel that had handholds cut out and regularly spaced along the sides. Frances appeared at the door with Papa Bear Clay in tow along with three of his friends who had agreed to carry the board up to the Center. *None of the oldsters could have done this on their own,* I thought as I watched them slide her from the bed which had been pushed back into its niche. They gently pulled her shrouded body over to the board which was sitting on a special gurney.

Frances pulled the hood over Ruth's face and they positioned themselves like a drill team ready to maneuver their cargo to the door. All of the residents had filed out to the central walkway in front of their respective homes carrying candles to light the dark night. As the gurney wheeled by they fell in line forming a procession of wavering lights as the old ones walked and hobbled along to follow the route they knew would one day be there for each of them.

The four men wheeled her up the ramp and into the Center to the team waiting to receive her. They had prepared a bed where she would stay for the next day and a half until transported by the funeral home to the cemetery. Once again, they shifted her, carefully sliding her from the shroud board onto the plastic mattress which was covered by towels.

This cleverly designed cot was hooked up to a body-length pad that circulated cold water under her to slow down decomposition. It had two big tubes that recycled water into an ice chest on the floor. The team's task was made easier by keeping the ice chest full as opposed to placing and replacing gel packs around her body.

Everyone had a job to do. The death doulas stayed behind to remove the bed linen and disinfect Ruth's house. While they scrubbed down Ruth's death bed, she would rest in the peace of the Community Center where shifts of two residents would sit with her body. They rotated shifts every two hours until daylight. At dawn two residents from the flower guild brought in colorful bouquets to place at each end of her shrouded body. I learned later that these flowers would be used at the burial ceremony.

They kept the candles burning all night and throughout the next day and night. Friends of Ruth from the outside community were invited to volunteer as sitters. They would rotate in shifts until the morticians came to pick up Ruth for her final trip to the cemetery where her husband and daughter were buried.

Oskar had been monitoring Ruth's decline. When I called him to say she had passed away, he immediately volunteered to take an early shift. Afterward, he stopped by my trailer on his way home. I gladly welcomed him into Ruth's house; the full teapot was on the warmer and he helped himself while he caught me up on the news from the mansion. He told me that Adrienne had gone to live with Carmen and Uri, that Lady Alyce was adjusting to her new home, and that he had gotten the final paperwork to adopt Ricky. They were still living in the bunkhouse and had a six-month contract to care for the grounds and the woods. I told him all that had happened with Ruth at the very end. Pausing on his way out the door he gave me a long hug; we agreed to stay in touch. I watched him walk away and thought, *There goes a good man. Someday our paths will cross again.*

The Playbook set out a routine: at every change of shift, from 8 am to 8 pm, the Band of Angels choir would perform a call-and-response of Swing Low Sweet Chariot. When they finished, one of the residents would tell a story about Ruth and the Band of Angels played the role of the Amen Corner to chime in with the community's appreciation. At noon, the entire community gathered for a memorial service led by Father Loren, who was Ruth's priest.

I watched one of the shift changes at 4 pm when I took my turn along with Emily. Her task as death doula was almost over and she had joined the ranks of the sitters. I was moved to tears to witness the joy and love that these old people poured out to embrace the death of one of their own. *Ruth would be so pleased*, I thought as I took my seat.

The violinist, Eddy, stepped up to finish the ceremony with the eerie and moving sounds of his instrument playing a wailing rendition of Amazing Grace. I thought of the cunning planning Beulah had put into establishing this ritual to have everyone participate in saying goodbye.

For the next two hours, I sat in mourning to honor Ruth's life and death. I had a copy of the Playbook at hand to read if I needed to know what to do. As time dragged by, I realized the value of this ancient Jewish practice of watching over the dead was to slow us down enough for reflection not only on the loss of a life but also on the aches and pains of being alive. My self-induced, pity party for my aching back was interrupted by a visit from the two morticians who had worked with Beulah to write the funeral part of the Playbook. They were here to meet with Frances to make arrangements for the transport of Ruth's body to the cemetery.

I watched as they talked with Frances. *They are a perfect yin/yang pair of morticians*, I mused,—*one tall, one short—one fair, one dark—one golden auburn, one raven black.* They had moved close to where we were sitting and I could easily eavesdrop on their conversation. The tall attractive woman introduced herself as Althea; she had golden auburn hair streaked with gray. I thought, *I'll bet she is the manager of the outfit.*

I overheard her say, "I wrote the Modern-Traditional section of the Playbook." As they continued talking, I turned to that section in the book to read, "The path forward begins with the mortician arriving soon after death to remove the body for transport to the funeral home where she will embalm, wash, groom, and dress your loved one to prepare for viewing, cremation, or burial. The funeral home will offer a choice of caskets, a room for a gathering, and, if desired, a viewing. They will coordinate with your choice of pastor for a service and will file the necessary paperwork for a death certificate. They will provide transportation by hearse to the grave yard where the cemetery sexton will coordinate arrangements for a grave side service with tent and chairs, prepare the site, and help lower the casket into a grave or a vault."

Glancing up to see what they were doing, I thought that her young counterpart couldn't have been more of a contrast. Her beautiful heart shaped face had a natural blush to it that contrasted with her glossy black hair. Emily had left her seat to introduce herself as one of the death doulas. "My name is Bethany," said the young woman. "I wrote the Home Funeral section in the Playbook." She was dressed completely in black and had the agile look of a cat burglar. I thought, *I'll bet she could extricate a body from any situation.*

As Emily told her story, blow-by-blow recounting each step of the washing experience, I turned to the section of the Playbook that Bethany had written. "Home Funeral & Natural Burial: our mission is to return the death experience to the family. We will help you every step of the way to recreate the home funeral experience. You will be trained in the art of preparing your loved one's body, washing, dressing, and shrouding. Most importantly, we will teach you the techniques of keeping the body cool for viewing. You may transport or we will come to help. You may dig the grave, or we will do it for you. You may have a pine box or a woven willow coffin. You may have a grave side service or not. You will be the director and we will help."

They offered two very different ways to handle a death in the family. I saw that Bethany's was a true alternative to modern society's hide-the-body funeral practices. *This has the potential to revolutionize the funeral industry. Her family-first approach to death compares to hospice's patient-first approach to dying; you do it on your own terms.*

Breaking up the conversation, they promised Frances that the hearse would arrive in the morning at 10 am. Bethany asked that everyone be ready to go so we could caravan to the cemetery. Before they left, she complimented us on the setting. Beaming like a proud parent at graduation ceremonies, she said, "You have created a sacred space here; we will recreate one by the grave side at the cemetery."

By 6 pm I was grateful to relinquish my seat to the next rotation of sitters. As I left the Center, I heard Eddy begin to play. The mournful sound followed me down the wide central walkway until I entered Ruth's house and closed the door behind me. The tiny house was completely still, completely empty of Ruth's presence. *She is not here, she is on her way to her final resting spot,* I thought. As I prepared leftovers for dinner, I hummed the Swing Low lyrics, "coming for to carry me home."

At one point, when she could still talk, Ruth asked me if I wanted to take over the house. I was tempted; it was such a beautiful space. But, I told her no, I needed to find my own, next home. But knowing this special place with this special community had given me a sense of homecoming, of being loved and nurtured. I felt so grateful to these old folks who had pioneered a community focused on end-of-life help. But, I knew I had many miles to travel before I was ready to be a resident here.

I spent the evening packing; my plan was to head north to my sister's home directly from the cemetery after the grave side service. My last task was to write the final advice column. I sat at the table, typing on my laptop in the gloomy light of the computer. When I emailed it to Adrienne, I encouraged her to visit Lady Alyce fearing that she might just offload that task to Carmen. *That's all I can do from here,* I thought and clicked shut my laptop.

As promised, the big black Cadillac hearse backed up to the side gate by the Community Center right at 10 am. All of the oldsters were gathered around, ready for a field trip. Bethany and Althea wheeled in a casket gurney with an intricately woven wicker coffin riding on top. They sidled up next to the metal cot. Emily had removed the ice chest cooling system moments before they arrived. Bethany directed us to gather around and grab hold of the top sheet. She said, "We are going to do a lift, shift, and hold." Pulling the sheet tight, we lifted Ruth's shrouded body up and shuffling together we moved to suspend her over the coffin. Bethany called out, "Now gently lower her—easy. There we go. Good!"

Ruth was nestled in the beautiful pale-blue quilted padding inside the coffin. Bethany reverently pulled the shroud's cowl around and over her face. Althea brought over one of the bouquets and we placed flowers all over her shrouded body. Bethany carefully closed the lid and fastened its wicker handles into the woven loops. We were ready to roll.

The two morticians guided the coffin down the ramp to the back of the Cadillac's rear door. Clay ushered everyone out to the mini-bus he had rented for the trip. I told him I would follow in my car. He called out, "Lock that back gate when you go out!" As I walked down the center path one last time, I thought of how much I had learned about aging and dying during my time with Ruth. All of my fears were gone—replaced by understanding and images of a community embracing death through love.

We caravanned our way to the cemetery, past farms and fields filled with sheep and lambs. We were heading for the Old Cox Butte Cemetery, 15 minutes out of town. I had been there twice before, once to help Ruth bury her husband and once to bury her daughter.

I pulled up behind the mini-bus; the hearse was situated close to the open gravesite. All of the oldsters were piling out of the bus, ushered by the Grand Pooh-Bah of cemetery sextons. He wore a pork pie hat at a jaunty angle and he used a sturdy wood cane. I heard him introduce himself to Clay as Donnie

Dove. *What a perfect name for a cemetery caretaker,* I thought. He worked the crowd making everyone comfortable in a reverent sort of way. I could see that the residents loved him. *He has street creds—he must be 80-something.*

Althea and Bethany stood at ease next to the yawning back of the hearse keeping an eye on Donnie to make sure he didn't steal the show. I noticed two young men standing off to the side leaning on their shovels. Bethany signaled for them to come forward. She had already enlisted Clay's help and gave him a pair of gloves matching her own. They took up positions opposite each other as they slid the wicker coffin out of the hearse. Walking in unison the three men and Bethany carried and placed the woven box on top of two planks spread over the open grave. Althea brought the remaining bouquet and carefully laid it on top.

Frances stepped up to read a letter from Ruth written especially for this event. She had been here before and knew what to say. Frances choked up at her admonition, "To all my friends, love life—it is precious." Since we had already done so much grieving, we were ready to move to the final step. Frances signaled Bethany to proceed. Working quickly, Bethany passed two ropes under the coffin.

The four took their positions. Standing tall, they lifted the coffin up enough for Althea to remove the two boards. Hand over hand, they slowly lowered it down to the bed of straw and wooden supports that waited at the bottom. I had read in the Playbook that the straw would speed decomposition and the wooden supports made pulling out the ropes easier. When she was all the way down, the residents actually cheered and clapped. I caught Bethany's eye and smiled at her astonished look. Beulah's Playbook had created ceremonies of respect which had spontaneously created a culture of joy.

Then it was over. The Cloud of Witnesses had accomplished their mission of caring for each other. Papa Bear Clay shepherded his precious charges into the bus with Donnie helping them navigate the stairs. The two men shook hands and the bus pulled away. I had said my goodbyes, planning to stay behind for a bit to walk the cemetery and pay my respects. Before she left, Bethany pointed to a woman who was working up on the hilltop. She said, "You mentioned you wanted to talk to the owner. Well, there she is."

Trudging part way up the hill, I turned and watched the Cadillac roll slowly out of the gate and glide down the road. *It is like a big, black land shark,* I thought. Puffing a bit by the time I reached the top, I paused to catch my breath. The woman Bethany had pointed out stopped raking and came over to introduce herself. "I am Sylvia." I asked, "The owner?" She nodded and said, "Yes, this is my farm and I am transitioning it back to its natural condition as much as possible." Her deep set eyes sparkled when she talked about the land. She was about my height with long gray hair pulled back and tied at her neck. Many hours of outside work had carved her beautiful face with lines and creases giving her a noble bearing. She wore a canvas coat with big pockets like the one that Oskar wore. *They are both gardeners in different ways,* I realized.

We strolled through the gravesites and she explained that she regarded the acreage as she would any ground, noting the slope of the hill, the erosion patterns, the condition of the trees. Stopping by one huge fir, she said, "Some of them are my problem children." She explained that these pioneer cemeteries needed care to protect the old graves and to recondition the ground to receive new burials. She told me they had reinstituted the community-old practice of natural burials twelve years earlier when her business purchased the land.

She showed me where she had added dirt to graves that had caved in and pointed out one marker that had fallen over. "Actually, the family owns the marker and it is their responsibility to care for it. If we can find them, we will send notification that this one needs help. There are so many 'lost' markers that we really need a group to befriend the cemetery on behalf of the families who no longer come to pay their respects. There is a lot to do!"

I thanked her for her time and for her service to preserve the history captured here. Gathering a few branches that lay on the ground, she said, "You should take a look around to see if there is a place you are interested in. If you don't see a marker or a tombstone, then that may be an open site." She waved as she went back to the top of the hill.

On my own with everyone gone, I meandered among the headstones looking at the old dates, names, and inscriptions. I came to a small clearing in the midst of the stones. The sun was out and I sat down on the ground. I surveyed the horizon from where I sat and saw three long mountain tops with woods on either side. I lay back with my hands behind my head feeling the blessed sun on my face and the warm earth at my back. I had a sudden recall of my husband's urn which was packed up at the POD self storage. The red hot flame of grief engulfed me. Even after all this time, I cried out loud.

Sitting up, I traced the line of the horizon. The bird song was the only sound breaking the silence. Right then and there, I decided to bring my husband's ashes here. I would talk to Donnie and buy the plots I was sitting on. I would ask for a small grave side service and spread his ashes directly into the soil to wait for the day when I would join him. Ever since I had seen Ruth's beautiful wicker coffin, I knew that would be the way I would go into the ground.

I lay back down to savor my decision. The clouds scudded through the blue sky. I had finally lain to rest my feeling of being lost—that awful feeling I had carried with me ever since the night in the hospital waiting room. I cried again for the hole in my past that never healed because I did not say goodbye to my dear husband's body the way I had with Ruth. He had been whisked away and cremated. No ritual, no reverential washing; only a formal memorial service and a small heavy metal box. It was not enough to heal the trauma of a heart attack in the dead of night.

Now, I felt certain that I had found our final resting spot. I could imagine my family gathered here taking comfort from this beautiful setting. I knew that I needed to anchor my husband's ashes to a gravesite in order for me to go on living. When I finally joined him, this would be the place where, together, our remains would ride the Earth's rotation until the end of time.

As I threaded my way back down the hill through the markers and stones, I realized that I felt whole again; I felt elated. I began to hum the words of Swing Low and by the time I reached my car I was singing at the top of my lungs.

Well, now I looked over Jordan,
And what did I see?
Comin' for to carry me home.
There was a band of angels,
Comin' after me.
Comin' for to carry me home!
Swing low, sweet chariot
Comin' for to carry me home.

What is the meaning of my life?

Dear Lady Alyce: I know that I speak for many of your readers when I offer my condolences on the loss of your fellow writer, Minnie. I have enjoyed your columns and treasure your advice. I have come to think differently about my own situation as I have tried to implement some of your suggestions. I am 84 years old and, after my wife's death last month, I am all alone in the world. I don't know why I am the one left behind—why I am still alive—but I figure I must have something left to do here on Earth. How do I truly know the meaning of my life?

—Wondering

Dear Wondering: Thank you for your condolences; Minnie was a loyal companion and I loved her dearly. You are asking a question that does not have a universal answer but has been universally asked by humans since the beginning of time. Asking this question as you get closer to death is a defining moment for every person. My dear friend, Minnie, taught me that answering this question and living by that answer can be the greatest achievement of a person's life. I am mortified to say that it took her death for me to realize what a good person she was.

Belief in a higher power is foundational to the religious systems that address the universal experience of living and dying. The central question to the great religions is, **What is the meaning of life?**

The **Hindus** would say: To act virtuously and righteously, live within moral and ethical grounds, obtain enjoyment from life, and seek enlightenment

The **Jews** would say: To fulfill the mission that God has given us through His Torah

The **Buddhist** community would say: To recognize the impermanence of all things and free oneself from attachment; to escape suffering through realizing the truth of Nirvana

The **Christians** would say: To love the Lord thy God with your whole heart, soul, mind, and strength, and to love thy neighbor as thyself

The **Muslims** would say: To know and
worship God through the Qur'an

Like those who have gone before us, we must seek answers to what we cannot
know from experience alone. A scientific world view will not give comfort; reason
alone tells us we are descending to a dark pit. The great scientist, Einstein, said,
"To know an answer to this question means to be religious."

I urge you, *Wondering,* to embrace your destiny and find the meaning that you
seek. You may think you are all alone, but our journey toward death is crowded
with others. You have only to look around to find your fellow oldsters at your
local senior center, church, or nursing home. Reach out to those who you can
help; reach out to those who will help you in making this final passage. Take
comfort from saying *yes* to life and live it fully until you cannot.

Six Companion Exercises to the Six Advice Columns

Embedded in the preceding novel are the six advice columns that the editorial team wrote on how to age with courage. In this appendix are six companion exercises that will help you implement the team's advice into your own life situation.

The six exercises will equip you:
- <u>to make decisions</u> through the ups and downs
  and unexpected pitfalls of aging
- <u>to gain clarity</u> on your end-of-life wishes.

The answers are neither right nor wrong; they are catalysts to your own insight.

These exercises are designed to help you make the decisions unique to your situation and changing circumstances. They are based on the stages of aging: **FRAGILITY, DECLINE, DISABILITY, FAILING HEALTH, ACTIVE DYING.** The exercises are designed to build on each other and will result in six tangible outcomes:

1. A description of your current level of capability (**Baseline A**),
2. The identification of **significant** others,
3. A contingency plan (**Baseline B**),
4. Reflections on **values** for aging and end-of-life **scenarios**,
5. A **decision tool** to help you fill out an Advanced Directive & POLST, and
6. Guidance on **funeral planning** for help in making after life arrangements.

We oldsters need to recognize that reaching an age where we care about the issues raised in the novel is, in itself, an accomplishment. We have lived lives full of stress and worry, of sadness and of joy. We have fended for ourselves, made decisions, loved and lost. We are a source of knowledge and wisdom. All our lives we have planned for the future—now—is no exception. As we reach this part of life's journey, we need to distill the lessons we have learned from our experience and apply them to our own end-of-life challenges.

TABLE:
EXERCISES AND OUTCOMES

EXERCISE	TOPIC	OUTCOME	PAGES
#1	STAGES OF AGING	DESCRIPTION OF CURRENT LEVEL OF ABILITY = BASELINE A	Pages 80-83
#2	FRAGILITY	IDENTIFICATION OF SIGNIFICANT OTHERS	Pages 84-86
#3	DECLINE	CONTINGENCY PLAN IN CASE OF ILLNESS/INJURY = BASELINE B	Pages 87-91
#4	DISABILITY	VALUES FOR END-OF-LIFE SCENARIOS	Pages 92-95
#5	FAILING HEALTH	DECISION TOOL TO FILL OUT ADVANCED DIRECTIVE & POLST	Pages 96-99
#6	ACTIVE DYING	GUIDANCE ON FUNERAL PLANNING	Pages 100-101

On my seventieth birthday
I felt as if I were standing on a mountain height,
at whose foot the ocean of eternity was audibly rushing;
while before me, life with its deserts and flower-gardens,
its sunny days and its stormy days, spread out green, wild, and beautiful.

Heinrich Zschokke

As you can see, the Stages of Aging (listed below) represent a progressive decline in health. Old age is not a diagnosis, but rather it is a gradual loss of resiliency. We are less able to withstand the effects of aging and less able to recover from disease, medical treatment, or injury.

Before we begin the exercises, you should circle the stage that best represents your <u>current</u> stage of aging. The list on the right hand side (Fears and Concerns) is **not** necessarily linked to a particular stage. For example, *loss of independence* might be a worry at every stage. Regardless of which stage you circled, find your <u>top three</u> Fears & Concerns and circle them.

STAGES OF AGING [1]	*COMMON FEARS & CONCERNS*
GOOD HEALTH (*Feeling the effects of aging*)	Loss of independence Loss of physical health Loss of mental health
FRAGILITY (*Susceptible to unintended treatment complications/fall*)	Loss of healthy baseline Inability to care for pets Loss of loved ones
DECLINE (*Focus on care not cure/ postpone disability*)	Loss of home Loss of routine Financial worries
DISABILITY (*Focus on coping emotionally/logistically*)	Fear of burden to others Loss of privacy Loneliness/Guilt
FAILING HEALTH (*Affairs in order*)	Fear of pain/suffering Despair/Fear of dying
ACTIVE DYING (*Avoid 911/accept Hospice*)	Question meaning of life Fear of being vulnerable

1 Butler, K. (2013). *Knocking on Heaven's door: The path to a better way of death.* NY: Scribner.

EXERCISE	TOPIC	OUTCOME	PAGES
#1	STAGES OF AGING	DESCRIPTION OF CURRENT LEVEL OF ABILITY/BASELINE = PLAN A	Pages 80-83

The first advice column in the novel (p. 19) addressed expectations for the unpredictable nature of life as we age. The editors gave the advice: 1) to create several contingency plans, 2) to find a role model for aging, and 3) to embrace mortality. This exercise focuses on **Contingency Plans** and will describe your current baseline of daily living activities. The concept of a baseline (Plan A) is important because it creates a reference point for future contingency plans.

CREATE <u>CURRENT</u> BASELINE = PLAN A   **Date completed_____**

NOTE: *the items with one asterisk* are one of the Activities of Daily Living (ADL) used to assess an individual's level of functioning to determine eligibility for insurance benefits. Items with two asterisks** are Instrumental Activities of Daily Living (IADL) which are used by medical personnel in conjunction with ADLs to assess when assistance is required.*

Circle a number to rank your **<u>own ability to perform</u>** the following activities.
1 = fully competent,
2 = competent but it takes longer than it used to,
3 = need help **(write in the name of who does this activity for you/or helps you)**

A) Manage Household:

Manage personal finances: ** 1   2   3_____

Use telephone: **   1   2   3_____

Access Transportation: **   1   2   3_____

Upkeep of Automobile: 1   2   3_____

Upkeep of Technology: 1   2   3_____

Answer correspondence: 1   2   3_____

Maintain contact w/family: 1   2   3_____

_____: 1   2   3_____

_____: 1   2   3_____

CONTINUE EXERCISE #1

Circle a number to rank your **own ability to perform** the following functions.

1 = fully competent,

2 = competent but it takes longer than it used to,

3 = need help (**write in the name of who does this activity for you/or helps you**)

B) Manage Current Home:

Housekeeping: **	1	2	3_____
Grocery Shop: **	1	2	3_____
Prepare Meals: **	1	2	3_____
Feed Yourself: *	1	2	3_____
Run Errands:	1	2	3_____
Laundry: **	1	2	3_____
Maintain Yard:	1	2	3_____
Care for Pets:	1	2	3_____
Take out trash:	1	2	3_____
_____:	1	2	3_____
_____:	1	2	3_____

C) Maintain Mobility:

Transfer bed/chair:*	1	2	3_____
Bathing:*	1	2	3_____
Dress w/o help:*	1	2	3_____
Maintain continence:*	1	2	3_____
Toileting/hygiene:*	1	2	3_____
_____:	1	2	3_____
_____:	1	2	3_____
_____:	1	2	3_____

CONTINUE EXERCISE #1

Circle a number to rank your **own ability to perform** the following functions.

1 = fully competent,

2 = competent but it takes longer than it used to,

3 = need help (**write in the name of who does this activity for you/or helps you**)

D) Manage Health:

Maintain mental acuity: 1   2   3_____

Manage medications: **   1   2   3_____

Manage doctor visits: 1   2   3_____

Exercise: 1   2   3_____

Stay safe: 1   2   3_____

Maintain balance: 1   2   3_____

_____: 1   2   3_____

E) Maintain Life Interests:

Spiritual Practice: 1   2   3_____

Travel: 1   2   3_____

Socialize: 1   2   3_____

Read/Research: 1   2   3_____

Create/Art: 1   2   3_____

Stay current/news: 1   2   3_____

Attend social events: 1   2   3_____

_____: 1   2   3_____

F) Care of Others:

Spouse/Partner: 1   2   3_____

Grandkids: 1   2   3_____

Friends: 1   2   3_____

Volunteer: 1   2   3_____

_____: 1   2   3_____

CONTINUE EXERCISE #1

G) Customized list of other activities that are important to you:

_____ :   1   2   3_____

_____ :   1   2   3_____

_____ :   1   2   3_____

_____ :   1   2   3_____

_____ :   1   2   3_____

_____ :   1   2   3_____

At this point in the exercises, we have created a record of your capabilities as of this date. This is important because we want to track the changes that occur as you age. In the future, making important medical decisions may require tradeoffs between treatment outcomes and life activities. This record will help you when questioning the physician who is trying to explain the risks versus benefits of a recommended treatment.

SUMMARY: the items with one asterisk* are one of the Six Activities of Daily Living (ADL) used to assess an individual's level of functioning to determine eligibility for insurance benefits.

Eating, Transfer bed/chair, Bathing, Dress w/o help, Maintain continence, Toileting/ hygiene

Items with two asterisks** are the eight Instrumental Activities of Daily Living (IADL) which are used in conjunction with ADLs to assess when assistance is required.

**Manage personal finances, Use telephone, Access Transportation, Housekeeping, Grocery Shop, Prepare Meals, Laundry, Manage medications*

EXERCISE	TOPIC	OUTCOME	PAGES
#2	FRAGILITY	IDENTIFICATION OF SIGNIFICANT OTHERS	Pages 84-86

The second advice column in the novel (p. 29) responded to the reader who broke her hip. They told her to: 1) change her attitude from anger to acceptance, 2) prepare herself for the forces of aging, and 3) cultivate relationships that are mutually helpful. This exercise focuses on mutually helpful relationships by identifying those people in your life who are significant.

We are going to use an imaginary situation to identify **significant others** in your life upon whom you rely, who are helping you, and whom you might be caring for. Let us consider your current living situation to be our baseline (Plan A). The following exercise will help you identify the levels of support **currently** in place to help you function at this level.

IDENTIFY SIGNIFICANT OTHERS
(PERSONAL AND PROFESSIONAL)

Imagine that you are driving downtown at noon **_today_** and you are in an accident that knocks you unconscious. You are taken to the hospital where you stay in a coma for 24 hours.

a) Who would be the first person (or animal) to feel the effects of you not returning home from your shopping trip? _____

_____

b) Based on your usual daily interactions **how long** would it be before someone realized you were not home from the shopping trip? _____

_____

c) Who is that someone (Name)? _____
What is their relationship to you? _____

d) If a police officer looked through your wallet could he/she easily find an emergency name and number to call?   Yes _____   No _____

e) If the police do find a notification number, whom would they call? _____

_____

f) Would that person (surrogate) know what to do to step in and take care of your immediate responsibilities at home (like feeding the pets or alerting relatives)?
Yes _____   No _____

CONTINUE EXERCISE #2

Have you spoken **lately** to this person about naming them as your emergency contact person?   Yes _____   No _____

ACTIONS:

1) Prepare an emergency contact card and place it in your wallet.

2) Verify that the numbers on your phone's emergency contact list show whom to call.

3) Speak to your surrogate(s) to clarify your expectations and their continued willingness to serve in this role.

4) Prepare a list of instructions for whomever would step up to help manage your household.

5) Post on your refrigerator a list of emergency contact names and numbers

What we learned from this exercise is who is in your innermost circle of activity and whom you trust to speak for you. Now, what we need to do is identify those who are in your life, outside of this first circle but close enough that they are concerned about you.

We will continue our imaginary situation by lengthening your stay in the hospital to one week and see what happens. The ripple effect of you not following your usual routine will be felt in your social group(s). In the section below, identify those who have a need to know **other than** the people you have mentioned above.

List in **order of importance** those you want informed that you are in the hospital for a week.

Name _____ Contact# _____ Relationship _____

_____#_____

_____#_____

_____#_____

_____#_____

_____#_____

_____#_____

_____#_____

_____#_____

CONTINUE EXERCISE #2

We are going to use a different imaginary situation to highlight risks at home that you can do something about. Imagine that **tonight**, you get up from bed to go to the bathroom and you trip and fall on the hallway rug. You cannot get up.

As you are lying on the floor in pain, who would be the first person to come to your aid? _____ Relationship _____

If you are ALONE in the house, where is your phone usually kept in relation to where you fell in the hallway?

Phone Location: _____

Distance to crawl: _____

If you called 911, who (other than you) would let them in the front door?

_____ Relationship _____

NOTE: One of the most important actions you can take is to stay on the line until the dispatcher tells you to hang up.

ACTION: Before anything actually happens:

1) Inspect your current pathway to the bathroom from the point-of-view of safety.

2) Remove any rugs or obstacles and install a nightlight if needed.

3) Consider hiding a key to the front door or placing it with a neighbor so that, if needed, you could tell the dispatcher how the first responders can enter your house in case you are unable to let them in.

4) Evaluate the location of your phone at night._

5) Keep by the phone a card with your name, address, security door code, and phone number of emergency contact person to use when talking to the dispatcher.

6) Consider installing a personal safety system that would give you access to 24/7 help. There are a variety of systems with a variety of services.

7) Consider installing grab bars in the bathroom and shower to avoid falling in the future.

EXERCISE	TOPIC	OUTCOME	PAGES
#3	DECLINE	CONTINGENCY PLAN IN CASE OF ILLNESS/INJURY = BASELINE B	Pages 87-91

The third advice column in the novel (p. 39) responded to the reader who suffered a mild stroke and was trying to decide whether or not to move near one of her children. Their advice was to decide what to do sooner rather than later because this sort of event is a signal that accommodations must be made to maximize the health she had recovered. Now is her chance to decide what sort of help she needs to maintain her independence and to not exacerbate her heart condition. In short, she needs to develop a new plan that helps her stave off disability as long as possible.

This exercise uses the imaginary scenario of a broken hip to make you think about what you would do if you lost mobility and needed to make accommodations. We will continue our earlier scenario with your fall in the hallway. After the first responders get you to the hospital, the emergency room physician finds that your femur and hip joint are badly damaged. Also, he diagnoses osteoporosis which will be a factor in your recovery prognosis because it is a chronic condition that has affected your bones. However, the immediate problem is logistical. Your broken hip is going to require surgery and a long recovery in a rehabilitation facility.

The doctor predicts that you will be in the facility for three weeks, in a wheelchair at home for an additional three, and may need a walker after that. He does not believe that you will ever fully recover from this fall. He tells you that you can regain mobility, but you must not expect to do what you used to be able to do.

Let us assume that for the purpose of this exercise, you have left the rehabilitation facility and are in a wheelchair when you return home. Try to imagine how your own ability to perform the daily living activities would have changed. Follow the instructions to circle the number that best represents your competency **when you are home in a wheelchair for an expected three weeks**.

Before you begin, go back to page 79. Based on the scenario of this exercise, circle any new fears you might have after your talk with the doctor.

CONTINUE EXERCISE #3

Circle a number to rank your **own ability to perform** the following activities after returning home and are **using a wheelchair for an expected three weeks.**
1 = fully competent,
2 = competent but it takes longer than it used to,
3 = need help **(write in who could help you with this activity: personal/professional)**

A) Manage Household:

Manage personal finances:**	1	2	3_____
Use telephone: **	1	2	3_____
Access Transportation: **	1	2	3_____
Upkeep of Automobile:	1	2	3_____
Upkeep of Technology:	1	2	3_____
Answer correspondence:	1	2	3_____
Maintain contact w/family:	1	2	3_____
_____:	1	2	3_____
_____:	1	2	3_____

B) Manage Current Home:

Housekeeping:**	1	2	3_____
Grocery Shop:**	1	2	3_____
Prepare Meals:**	1	2	3_____
Feed Yourself:*	1	2	3_____
Run Errands:	1	2	3_____
Laundry: **	1	2	3_____
Maintain Yard:	1	2	3_____
Care for Pets:	1	2	3_____
Take out trash:	1	2	3_____
_____:	1	2	3_____
_____:	1	2	3_____

CONTINUE EXERCISE #3

Circle a number to rank your **own ability to perform** the following activities after returning home and are **using a wheelchair for an expected three weeks.**

1 = fully competent,

2 = competent but it takes longer than it used to,

3 = need help (**write in who could help you with this activity: personal/professional**)

C) Maintain Mobility:

Transfer bed/chair:*	1	2	3_____
Bathing:*	1	2	3_____
Dress w/o help:*	1	2	3_____
Maintain continence:*	1	2	3_____
Toileting/hygiene:*	1	2	3_____
_____:	1	2	3_____
_____:	1	2	3_____

D) Manage Health:

Maintain mental acuity:	1	2	3_____
Manage medications:**	1	2	3_____
Manage doctor visits:	1	2	3_____
Exercise:	1	2	3_____
Stay safe:	1	2	3_____
Maintain balance:	1	2	3_____
_____:	1	2	3_____

E) Maintain Life Interests:

Spiritual Practice:	1	2	3_____
Travel:	1	2	3_____
Socialize:	1	2	3_____
Read/Research:	1	2	3_____
Create/Art:	1	2	3_____
Stay current/news:	1	2	3_____
Attend social events:	1	2	3_____

CONTINUE EXERCISE #3

Circle a number to rank your **own ability to perform** the following activities after returning home and are **using a wheelchair for an expected three weeks.**
1 = fully competent,
2 = competent but it takes longer than it used to,
3 = need help (**write in who could help you with this activity: personal/professional**)

F) Care of Others:

Spouse/Partner:	1	2	3_____
Grandkids:	1	2	3_____
Friends:	1	2	3_____
Volunteer:	1	2	3_____
_____:	1	2	3_____

G) Customized list of other activities that are important to you:

_____:	1	2	3_____
_____:	1	2	3_____
_____:	1	2	3_____
_____:	1	2	3_____

Some of the people you marked after the #3 will be professionals, e.g. home health, meals on wheels, your accountant, housekeeper, and/or gardener. Some of the people you marked will be a significant other, relative, friend, or neighbor. Your inability to keep up your responsibilities will be shifted to them during the time you are using a wheelchair.

Exercise #3 is designed for comparison and contrast to exercise #1. Your task is to evaluate which living activities are the most important for **you to keep doing** (or **resume doing**) in the aftermath of your injury. Will you keep in place the people who have been helping you? Will you consider moving to where you have less responsibility and more assistance?

Use the template on the following page to record those insights which will guide your decisions in making new plans as your health changes.

CONTINUE EXERCISE #3

Compare the answers you gave in exercise #1 (pp. 80-83) to the answers you gave in exercise #3 (pp. 87-90). List the most important activities from each category and record your insights on the quality of life issues you value the most.

A) Manage Household:

B) Manage Current Home:

C)Maintain Mobility:

D) Manage Health:

E) Maintain Life Interests:

F) Care of Others:

G) List of other activities that are important to you:

EXERCISE	TOPIC	OUTCOME	PAGES
#4	DISABILITY	VALUES FOR END-OF-LIFE SCENARIOS	Pages 92-95

The fourth advice column in the novel (p. 51) was written to the husband who was suffering because he missed his wife so much. The advice suggested a way for him to transform his suffering by realizing that by bearing the burden of surrogate he had saved his wife from unnecessary pain. This is a big deal if you think about how dependent she was on him to say what was right for her because she could no longer make decisions. His values of **loyalty** and **commitment** guided him through her devolving process of disability, failing health and active dying. We notice that his end-of-life goal for her was not to buy more time but, instead, to ensure comfort care by putting in place systems of support at home.

The purpose of this exercise is to help you identify the values that guide people through decisive moments. (A value is defined for this activity as a person's principles or standards of behavior; one's judgment of what is important in life.)

SOME EXAMPLES OF VALUES TO GUIDE END-OF-LIFE DECISIONS: choose quality of life, choose length of life, follow physician's recommendation, let nature take its course, do what is best for my family, do what is best for me, willingness to accept help, strive to be independent, not be a burden, not deplete financial resources, courage to decide, accept responsibility for putting affairs in order, rely on self, rely on family, rely on God, achieve spiritual peace.

**Your task is to choose the values from the preceding list
(or supply your own) that you think drove the decisions
of the patients in the following scenarios.**

A) This scenario is from the book, *Being Mortal* by Atul Gwande (2014).

The patient is in his 60s and is suffering from incurable lung cancer. No matter what treatment he received, he had only months to live. The patient tells the physician, "Don't you give up on me. You give me every chance I've got" (p. 4).

Note: even though the eight-hour operation was technically a success, the patient never recovered from the complications and was on a ventilator for 14 days before his son gave approval for the team to stop. Dr. Atul's regret is that while he made certain the patient understood the risks of the procedure, he never discussed the larger truth about the patient's condition—that he would never return to the level of health he had even a few weeks earlier.

CONTINUE EXERCISE #4

What value(s) did the patient act on?_____

Looking back, we can see that his condition was terminal; the treatment only delayed his death by two weeks and imposed a good deal of suffering. His agreement to go forward with the treatment robbed him of any chance of dying outside of the hospital. Instead, his decision put both him and his son through great trauma.

> B) This scenario is from the book, *Knocking on Heaven's Door: The path to a better way of death,* by Katy Butler (2013).

This 85 year-old patient had a Do-Not-Resuscitate (DNR) bracelet and had decided she did not want to undergo heart surgery. However, when she had a heart attack, she was taken to the hospital where she recovered after a few days in intensive care. They gave her a cardiac catheterization which injects dye into her arteries to see the heart vessels. The test showed narrowed heart vessels.

They recommended coronary artery bypass grafts plus the two valve replacement surgery that she'd rejected earlier when she had a far better chance of surviving open-heart surgery. The patient said, "It's hard to give up hope" (p. 246) when she again decided against the surgery. Her daughter and sons supported her decision; she was released from the hospital to return home with help from hospice where she died peacefully within a couple of months.

What value(s) guided the patient in her second refusal of surgery? _____

_____

What value(s) guided the grown children in their support of her decisions? _____

_____

> C) This scenario is from *tuesdays with Morrie* by Mitch Albom (1997).

In his late 70s, Morrie was diagnosed with amyotrophic lateral sclerosis (ALS) which is a progressively debilitating disease. This book became famous because it chronicled Morrie's attitude in living with this terrible disease that has no cure. At the time of this quotation, Albom describes how he could still move.

"I asked Morrie if he felt sorry for himself."

"Sometimes, in the morning," he said. "That's when I mourn. I feel around my body, I move my fingers and my hands—whatever I can still move and I mourn what I've lost. I mourn the slow, insidious way in which I'm dying. But then I stop mourning."

CONTINUE EXERCISE #4

"Just like that?"

"I give myself a good cry if I need it. But then I concentrate on all the good things still in my life. On the people who are coming to see me. On the stories I'm going to hear. On you if it's Tuesday. Because we're Tuesday people."

"I grinned. Tuesday people."

"Mitch, I don't allow myself any more self-pity than that. A little each morning, a few tears, and that's all" (pp. 56-57).

What value(s) guided Morrie in his attitude to accepting ALS? _____

D) As critical decisions arise, we will make them based on our values. Enduring values act as a personal compass to keep us heading toward our end-of-life goals. We need to know ahead of time what makes our life worth fighting for or not. As the stakes get higher, we may need to "stick to our guns" if our first decision gets challenged by a new set of circumstances like a complication or a second opinion with a different calculation of the risks versus the benefits. Life can be messy and may get messier as we age toward death.

Unique to each of us will be the emergence of one condition or another which will claim our life. Will we know it when we see it? Decisive moments can be hidden within innocuous events, so we must heighten our awareness of our increased susceptibility to unintended consequences of medical treatments. Our task is to calibrate the risks of recovery as we are given information about the tradeoffs versus the benefits of a procedure or treatment.

At some point, we will be faced with a decision that is a defining moment. This will be one of those "fork in the road" type decisions. We must choose one way or the other. Inaction will have its own consequences because life marches on. If we can identify our values for end-of-life living, then we will have a guiding star to help us make decisions.

At this point in the exercise, list the values you hold dear as you near the end of life's journey:

_____

_____

_____

_____

_____

CONTINUE EXERCISE #4

E) In the novel, Frances tells Maggie of the yoga teacher who helps them learn to meditate. "He says we have to imagine the landscape surrounding our exit from this world and visualize ourselves in it ahead of time."

Our values serve as guideposts through the landscape on our way to the death scenario we envision. Scenarios can be very general (**I want to be pain-free no matter what**) or very specific (**die in my sleep in my own bed surrounded by family**).

DESCRIBE your ideal scenario surrounding your death:

EXERCISE	TOPIC	OUTCOME	PAGES
#5	FAILING HEALTH	DECISION TOOL TO FILL OUT ADVANCED DIRECTIVE & POLST	Pages 96-99

The fifth advice column in the novel (p. 61) listed the definitions of various legal documents that are designed to help you put your affairs in order while you are alive. These forms cannot be filled out after your death. For example, your failure to create a will leaves your family and friends unable to access your belongings and unable to settle your affairs until probate court (which can be expensive). Using these legal forms (which may vary by state) ensures that your wishes will be honored after your death. Our legal system provides the continuity to enact your wishes for your physical, medical, and financial affairs.

This exercise focuses on the Advanced Directive (AD) which is one of the most helpful documents for your caregivers and, usually, one of the most difficult to fill out. However, the answers from the last exercise will give you a good head start toward creating a sound AD based on your values and end-of-life goals. Once you fill out the AD, you will more easily fill out the POLST (Physician **Orders** for Life Sustaining Treatment). Those patients who have filled out an AD will be prepared to have the POLST conversation with their physician who must sign the POLST form to turn your wishes into medical orders. The POLST order tells medical professionals what care is authorized by your physician.

The AD and the POLST are closely related but are used differently. For example, you cannot use a POLST form to name a surrogate. You can only do that with an Advance Directive.

ADs are typically hard to locate in an emergency situation, but since the POLST is a medical order, a copy should be in your medical chart. It is a brightly colored one-page form and can be kept posted on your refrigerator for easy access. Remember that emergency medical service (EMS) personnel cannot follow your Advance Directive during an emergency but they can follow a physician-signed POLST form. Because our health care system functions within a culture of "fix it at any cost" we must assert our right to end-of-life care without intervention, if we don't want to be "fixed." The POLST will do that!

We are best served by beginning this exercise with an understanding of what is death. Except in rare circumstances, **a person is declared dead when an irreversible cessation of circulation, respiration, and brain function occurs.**

As our life-sustaining systems give out, we are less and less able to make our wishes known; the legal forms guide those around us by clearly stating our wishes. We can see immediately that the experience is going to be very different for the

CONTINUE EXERCISE #5:

dying person than for those who are caregivers. Having the courage to grapple with these issues proactively—while we can—is a final gift to those who are trying to help us achieve our end-of-life goals.

You will notice that the questions on the Advance Directive are aimed at extracting information from you for the explicit purpose of stating your wishes. The AD is your friend!

For the first part of this exercise, we will recall the five stages of aging to give us reference points: FRAGILITY, DECLINE, DISABILITY, FAILING HEALTH, **ACTIVE DYING.** Filling out the AD form is going to require us to imagine that we are in the final stage. We might get there slowly as a result of natural aging or earlier than expected because of a procedure gone wrong, an untreatable disease, or an accidental, life-threatening injury. Regardless of how we get there, we must grapple with the issues of life-sustaining treatment.

One important factor in making decisions will be your medical baseline before an event happens. One special condition before consenting to treatment or to a recommended procedure is to get an answer to the question: "What are my chances of recovering my baseline?" This concept will help you and/or your surrogate in making decisions. The other concepts that will help you are your values and your ideal end-of-life scenario (p. 95).

ADVANCE DIRECTIVES focus on the activities of LIFE SUPPORT. "Life support refers to any medical means for maintaining life, including procedures, devices, and medications. If you refuse life support, **you will still get routine measures to keep you clean and comfortable.**"

So, the first thing to realize is that the AD is used when you cannot speak for yourself. When a decision must be made to keep you from an irreversible cessation of circulation, respiration, and/or brain function, what do you want to happen? You get to state your wishes by filling out the AD. The AD requires that you appoint a surrogate and, also, allows for the appointment of an alternative surrogate. Remember, the surrogate(s) may not act for you unless you become unable to make your own decisions.

Most AD forms include general information that will aid your conversation with your surrogate(s). Just as you would take the time to meet with an attorney to fill out a will, so should you take the time to meet with the person who agrees to be there for you when you need this very special help. The more you can talk about your goals and values, the better able your surrogate will be to make these tough decisions. Now is the time to give them the help and support that you will not be able to give when the time comes for them to decide for you.

CONTINUE EXERCISE #5:

Remember to have your surrogate sign both the AD and the POLST. You will need a witness to the signing by you and your surrogate (this may vary by state). This is an important legal document and should be kept where it is easily accessible. Make certain your surrogate has a copy. The POLST must then go to your primary care physician for his/her signature. Note: the AD does NOT get signed by the physician.

Use the following scenarios to choose the treatment you would select if you could speak for yourself. By completing this exercise, you will be ready to fill out both the Advanced Directive **AND** the POLST. Remember, it is the signed POLST that activates your wishes into medical orders. These orders are absolutely necessary to guide your care, especially in an emergency situation.

Because the forms may vary by state, you will need to make certain you have the correct forms. Most physicians' offices as well as hospitals make them available to their patients.

CONDITION	CIRCLE YOUR CHOICE OF TREATMENT
You have no pulse **and** are not breathing:	Attempt CPR –OR– Do not resuscitate (DNR)
You have a pulse **and/or** are breathing:	Comfort measures only –OR– Limited interventions (no intubation/no intensive care) –OR– Full treatment
You are ill, and the physician has to decide whether to order antibiotics or not:	NO (use other methods) –OR– Limited use –OR– YES (as medically indicated)
You are unable/unwilling to eat, and the physician has to decide to give you nutrition by feeding tube:	NO – OR– Define trial period –OR– Approve long-term use

Note: The choices for treatment (listed above) will have additional detail spelled out on the actual form(s).

Remember that hospice care is available for you once your physician determines that you are in need of comfort care rather than curative treatment. When discussing the POLST with your physician, you should include a discussion of hospice care to make certain your physician knows of your attitude toward accepting end-of-life comfort care. Follow up your talk with your physician by telling your surrogate what you discussed to insure your intentions are followed if you cannot speak for yourself.

EXERCISE	TOPIC	OUTCOME	PAGES
#6	ACTIVE DYING	GUIDANCE ON FUNERAL PLANNING	Pages 100-101

The sixth, and final, advice column in the novel (p. 75) urged the writer to embrace his destiny, find meaning, and live his life fully all the way to its end. This exercise stretches our imagination beyond the end. It asks us to consider how our passing out of life will affect others.

Just as the medical industry exists to provide health care, so does the funeral industry exist to provide death care. And, just as we used the advanced directive to state our wishes for end-of-life care, so can we use funeral planning to describe our wishes for care after death. Funeral homes usually have planning guides that describe the services they provide. By making key decisions ahead of time, you can put in place a process that will guide your loved ones through the maze of choices they will face upon your death. Grieving family and friends who arrive to find some of these decisions already made and some arrangements in place will be relieved of a burden at a time when they are least able to bear it. Pre-planning some of your own funeral is the final gift you can give them.

What happens to life's energy at death is a mystery and has been the subject of thought and discussion for thousands of years. Whether called spirit, soul, animus, atman, consciousness, or spiritual being, its journey is one of life's deepest mysteries and is beyond the scope of this exercise on funeral planning which is concerned only with the body's journey.

The cessation of life triggers the process of death which will reduce the body to its biological components. How do you want your body to return to dust? Should you choose a natural burial? Should you choose cremation? Should you choose embalming? While you are able, you should make as many choices as you can. For those who choose to die at home, their family members and friends might be involved from the start.

The one decision that may give your loved ones the most help is whether or not you will be buried. You may want the comfort of knowing where your remains will be laid to rest. If you are a member of a family that already holds a burial plot, then this question may be settled for you by your ancestors. If not, then you might be the family member who wants to establish a family plot. One of the great benefits of a gravesite is the physical setting where family and friends will gather to say goodbye to you. The landscape of monuments, tombstones, and plaques, sets the stage for appropriate reflection on death. Many years later, descendants, perhaps unknown to you now, may come to find your grave as they seek to understand the mystery of their own lives. You have a chance to reach across time to them through the epitaph you create for your grave marker. While the obituary (newspaper notice) and the eulogy (brief speech at the service) are given within the first stages of your body's journey, the epitaph abides for a very long time. These short sayings are what draw visitors to wander through graveyards after paying homage to their own departed.

Related to this decision is the choice of a funeral home to help you with pre-planning and to help guide your family when they begin to grapple with the decisions triggered by your death. The funeral director becomes the living link between the plan you create and those who come to finalize arrangements. You will have been there before them and they will understand the importance of you thinking about them going through their loss of you.

Consider your funeral pre-planning as a precious opportunity for you to hold in your mind each person who will grieve your loss. This mental preparation will help you embrace the end-of-life scenario you imagined in earlier exercises.

A common practice is the writing of a will to empower others to settle your affairs. An old-time tradition that once accompanied the legal will was the ***ethical will*** which addressed non-legal issues. This was a practice of writing a "goodbye" letter. Often this letter was accompanied by a special gift—an heirloom—that you wish to pass on to favored family members and friends.

You can minimize the loss your death causes by using the letter to memorialize the link between younger family members and the older ones you remember. For example, you might tell a grandchild how they remind you of a great grandparent. You can use the letter to leave an enduring reassurance to your own children or to your friends. You might capture a family story by documenting it in a letter. A letter from a beloved person who has died is a treasure that can be accessed through all the stages of bereavement and long into the future. At some point, the reader will become the same age as you, the writer, and may take great comfort from the model you have set. Unlike the formal reading of a will, this informal communication can offer your family and friends a way to focus on life beyond grieving. Just as you found a surrogate to help you with the advance directive, you will need a surrogate to deliver your final gifts.

ACKNOWLEDGEMENTS

T hank you to my editors, each of whom offered their valuable insight, time, and perspective from their life experiences and from their stage of aging.

Cynthia Beal, Natural Cemeterian
Founder of the Natural Burial Company (age 60)

Dr. Timothy M. Bergquist
Professor Emeritus, Quantitative Analysis (age 68)

Dr. Michael H. Kennedy
Professor Emeritus Business and Management (age 72)

Len Hockley
Former member of Order of the Ecumenical Institute (age 82)

Phyllis Hockley
Former member of Order of the Ecumenical Institute (age 85)

Susan Maggs-Qualls
Retired CFO & Treasurer of Stony Court HOA (age 75)

Bonnie Temple, MA, NCC
Senior Enrollment Advisor RN/BSN Program @ NCU (age 66)

Bethany Wozniak, MS
Funeral Director (age 33)

FIELD TESTERS

Once I had the novel written, I went on to write the exercises. This reminded me of writing curriculum for my college classes. Over many years of teaching, I have learned that the best assignments become the ones the students get a chance to shape by giving the professor feedback. I was very blessed to find 19 people willing to field test the six exercises that accompany the advice columns. I was astonished at the depth of insight offered by my field testers. This book is much better for all of the input I received. Additionally, I give special thanks to those editors who did double duty by also completing the exercises.

Thank you to: Lyla Becker, Tim Bergquist, June Campbell, Loren Crow, Hannah Dean, Patty Murphy-Gelardi, Michael Kennedy, Len Hockley, Phyllis Hockley, Joan Maggs, Sue Maggs-Qualls, Patti Meneely, Bob Meneely, Sharon Ogle, Roberta O'Neal, Ruth Raisler, Ani Sinclair, Karen Smith, and Bonnie Temple

Special mention: Valerie Laurita/Clark for guidance at the start of the project, Linda Magyary for cover photos, Connie Kennedy for her encouragement, and my husband, Chuck Foster, for his unflagging support.

FINAL STEPS

After all of the input and all of the suggestions from editors and field testers, the dragon at the editorial gate became the book's best arbiter. A former student of mine, Brittany Hanania, polished the manuscript as she would a master's thesis. I am thankful that her young eyes scrutinized the grammar, watched for internal consistency, and completed overall preparation for publication. Yes, I am grateful for her help. More than that, I am uplifted that she has surpassed her teacher. I lay claim to all errors since I was the final proofreader.

Finally, I thank Luminare Press and crew for their diligent guidance and support.

References

Albom, M. (1991). *tuesdays with Morrie*. NY: Doubleday.

Baines, K. (2006). *Ethical wills (2nd* Ed.). Cambridge, MA: Da Capo Press.

Butler, K. (2013). *Knocking on heaven's door: The path to a better way of death.* NY: Scribner.

Callanan, M. & Kelley, P. (1992). *Final gifts: Understanding the special awareness, needs, and communications of the dying.* NY: Bantam.

De Beauvoir, S. (1965). *A very easy death.* NY: Random House.

Doughty, C. (2017). *From here to eternity: Traveling the world to find the good death.* NY: W.W. Norton & Company, Inc.

Frankl, V. (1985). *Man's search for meaning.* NY: Simon & Schuster, Inc.

Gawande, A. (2014). *Being mortal.* NY: Metropolitan Books.

Kalanithi, P. (2016) *When breath becomes air.* NY: Random House.

Kubler-Ross, MD. E. (1982). *On life after death.* Berkeley, CA: Celestial Arts.

Kubler-Ross, MD. E. (1969). *On death and dying.* NY: MacMillan Publishing Co.

Moore, T. (1992). *Care of the soul: A guide for cultivating depth and sacredness in everyday life.* NY: HarperCollins Publishers, Inc.

Nearing, H. (1995). *Light on aging and dying.* Gardiner, ME: Tilbury House.

Tolstoy, L. (2017). *The death of Ivan Ilyich.* San Bernardino, CA: Tribeca Books.

Wilde, C. (2017). *Confessions of a funeral director: How the business of death saved my life.* NY: HarperCollins Publishers.

Wiman, C. (2013). *My bright abyss: Meditation of a modern believer.* NY: Farrar, Straus and Giroux.

ADDITIONAL RESOURCES

Advance Care Planning-NHDD:
www.nhdd.orgpublic-resources/

The Natural Burial Company:
www.naturalburialcompany.com/

National Hospice and Palliative Care Organization:
www.nhpco.org